Society of Friends New England Yearly Meeting

Doctrines, Christian Advices, and Rules of Discipline of New England

Yearly Meeting of Friends

Society of Friends New England Yearly Meeting

Doctrines, Christian Advices, and Rules of Discipline of New England
Yearly Meeting of Friends

ISBN/EAN: 9783337158989

Printed in Europe, USA, Canada, Australia, Japan

Cover: Foto ©Lupo / pixelio.de

More available books at **www.hansebooks.com**

DOCTRINES,

CHRISTIAN ADVICES,

AND

RULES OF DISCIPLINE

OF

NEW ENGLAND

YEARLY MEETING OF FRIENDS.

PRINTED BY DIRECTION OF THE MEETING.

NEW BEDFORD:
E. ANTHONY & SONS, PRINTERS.
1872.

INTRODUCTION.

The first notices on the records of New England Yearly Meeting, of any rules of Discipline for the observance of its members, appear in the minutes of that meeting in the years 1708 and 1709.

The Discipline then adopted consisted of twenty Articles, with an Introduction, declaring it to be the duty of all Friends "to walk in the self-denying way of Truth in all humility and plainness, having regard to the early testimonies of many worthy elders against pride, covetousness, and superfluity of every sort," quoting 1st Peter i. 14, 15; Rom. xii. 2; Phil. iv. 8, 9. And the quarterly meetings were directed to recommend these articles to the monthly meetings, "to be given in charge to such Friends as are chosen to visit families, that they may see that Friends live up to Truth's testimony, in these, and in all other respects."

They are designated as "what was agreed on for ye better regulating of Friends in their deportment, and apparel, etc., at our Yearly Meeting held at Newport ye 14th 4 [6] mo., 1708, with some correction at our Yearly Meeting for business held at Newport on Rhode Island ye 13th of ye 4 [6] mo., 1709."

In 1733, the subject of the Discipline was again before the meeting, and in 1734 a committee was appointed "to consider said minutes and make such remarks toward alterations as they may think needful, and return the same to our next Yearly Meeting, and collect what they may think proper from the minutes of Pennsylvania Yearly Meeting."

In 1735, the committee reported "that some of the minutes of Pennsylvania Yearly Meeting may be profitably introduced." The committee refer to the minutes agreed to by the Yearly Meeting in 1709, and conclude that it is not expedient to alter these, but rather, in tender Christian love, to recommend their observance.

1736. "Our friend John Hammet is appointed and desired to transcribe the whole of our minutes respecting the regulating Friends in their church government or discipline, deportment, etc.—that is to say—one copy for each monthly meeting belonging to this Yearly Meeting, and our friend Clark Rodman as treasurer is to pay for the same."

No copy of this collection has been found.

At the Yearly Meeting in 1760, a committee was appointed "to revise and collect the whole of the Yearly Meeting's minutes for Discipline, and also to peruse the English book of Discipline, and also that of Pennsylvania, and extract such parts, in order to join with ours, as they shall judge necessary, and lay the whole before this meeting for approbation." The following report was presented to the same meeting, viz.: "We, your committee appointed to collect and revise a set of Rules for Church Discipline throughout this Yearly Meeting, having several times met and considered the same, do report that the Rules of our Friends of old England are suitable for us with the following remarks." (Here follow nine proposed variations from the English Discipline.)

"This meeting therefore appoints the following committee to agree with some suitable person or persons, to transcribe two copies more of the English Book of Discipline, one for each quarterly meeting, to be paid out of the Yearly Meeting stock, and see that the several paragraphs brought in by the committee are carefully entered under their proper heads. And this meeting recommends to each quarterly meeting, that they furnish each particular of their monthly meetings with transcripts of the same, for the use intended, and that the same be done as soon as possible."

1783. "The matter of revising the Discipline is committed to the meeting for sufferings, with such women Friends as may be appointed by the women's meeting, to report their progress to our next Yearly Meeting."

1785. "The meeting for sufferings having gone through the revisal of our Discipline, and laid a digest thereof before this meeting for its disposal, after solidly and weightily considering thereon, it is concluded to commit it to our friends, Edward Shove and others, who are to unite with the meeting for sufferings and the committee the women may appoint, to consider thereof, and make alterations and amendments, if any may appear necessary, and report to an adjournment of this meeting."

At a subsequent session, the same year, the following minute was made, viz.:

"The committee to consider of the Discipline made a report which is to the satisfaction of this meeting, and is as follows: We, your committee respecting the proposed Discipline, have met with the members of the meeting for sufferings, and heard it read, and with such alterations as are now made are easy therewith, and submit the disposal thereof to the Yearly Meeting.

"For the committee. PAUL GREENE.
CATHARINE ALMY.

"And the said digest as it now stands is adopted as the Rules of Discipline for this Yearly Meeting, and the communicating of it to the quarterly and monthly meetings is committed to the care and oversight of the meeting for sufferings, in such manner as may appear best."

The work was printed the same year under the title of "The Book of Discipline agreed on by the Yearly Meeting of Friends for New

England. Containing extracts of minutes, conclusions, and advices of that meeting, and of the Yearly Meetings of London, Pennsylvania and New Jersey, and New York, from their first institution. Alphabetically arranged. Providence, [in small quarto,] 1785."

1807. In this year, twenty-two years after the publication of the first printed edition of the Book of Discipline, — "during which period the new regulations which had taken place having rendered it an imperfect collection of the rules of the Society, and the book being out of print, the Yearly Meeting committed the revisal of our Discipline to the meeting for sufferings, and that meeting having with care and diligence completed and laid the same before the Yearly Meeting in the sixth month, 1809," — it was adopted and directed to be printed.

The title was now changed to "Rules of Discipline of the Yearly Meeting held on Rhode Island for New England. Printed by direction of the meeting. New Bedford: Abraham Shearman, Jr., printer. 1809."

Reprints, with the same title, and such additions as had been directed by the Yearly Meeting, were issued in 1826, 1840, 1846, and 1856.

In all the issues of the Book of Discipline to this time, the advices were given with little variation from the original phraseology, and the date of issue was appended to each paragraph.

1868. The consideration of a revision of our Discipline again engaged the attention of the Yearly Meeting at its session this year, and a large committee of men and women Friends were appointed, to give the subject their careful attention, and report such changes as they might think proper to the next Yearly Meeting.

1871. The committee having been continued in appointment until this year, they then reported as follows, viz.:

"The joint committee appointed in 1868 to revise the Book of Discipline have given careful attention to the subject, which involved much time and labor; a different arrangement of the book having been early agreed upon as desirable.

"A statement of the fundamental belief and Doctrines of our society is first introduced, which is followed by Advices on Christian Practice, embracing in substance much that has been from time to time issued by this meeting. The Rules which have appeared necessary in the administration of the Discipline are then stated. We trust the system proposed is in accordance with the principles which have ever been maintained by our religious society, and that it is founded on the doctrines and precepts of the New Testament.

"An earnest desire has, we believe, been prevalent with the committee to seek for best help in the performance of this important duty, and the result of our labors is now submitted, with the hope that it may prove satisfactory to Friends."

The Yearly Meeting directed the document then presented and read, to be referred back to the same committee, " requesting them to make such changes and alterations, as, in their judgment, may be important to accomplish the concern of the meeting; and to cause an edition of five hundred copies to be printed in a pamphlet form, and sent down to our monthly meetings for distribution, as soon as practicable, in order that all Friends may have an opportunity to examine the work, and make any suggestions they may desire, to the committee, which they are encouraged to be prompt in doing."

1872. The committee on the Discipline reported as follows:

"The joint committee on the revision of the Book of Discipline report, that, as directed at our last Yearly Meeting, they have procured the printing of five hundred copies of the essay presented at that time, after some revision. These copies were distributed in the usual proportions among Friends in the several quarterly meetings, with a request that they should be returned, with comments, in season for further consideration by the committee, previous to a final revision and report. The work now presented is the result of this subsequent examination and review, and is submitted to the disposal of the Yearly Meeting."

The work, as then submitted, was read and considered during four joint sessions of the Yearly Meeting, and was, with some modifications, adopted. At the fifth joint session the following minute was made, viz.:

"The several articles which have been adopted by this meeting have now become its Discipline, and our subordinate meetings are directed to be governed by its provisions, when official copies of this minute are received by them, and also copies of the work."

Four Friends were appointed "to cause an edition of one thousand copies to be printed in good plain type, and to furnish all our subordinate meetings with the number of copies required for their use; the remainder of the edition to be placed in the hands of the treasurer of the meeting, to be sold to our members at cost."

In accordance with this direction of the Yearly Meeting this book has been printed.

CONTENTS.

CHAPTER I. CHRISTIAN DOCTRINE.

	PAGE.
From an epistle addressed by George Fox and others to the Governor of Barbadoes, 1671	3
From a Declaration of Christian Doctrine given forth by the Society of Friends, 1693	4
From the London General Epistle, 1736	8
From the Testimony of the Society of Friends, on the Continent of America	9
Of the Holy Scriptures	14

CHAPTER II. CHRISTIAN PRACTICE.

MEETINGS FOR WORSHIP	16
PRIVATE RETIREMENT AND PRAYER	20
Reading the Holy Scriptures	22
On Gifts and Services for the Religious Benefit of Others	23
On Simplicity, Moderation, and Self-Denial	26
Love and Unity, Part I	29
Part II	31
Liberality and Benevolence	32
Advice in Relation to the Ministry	34
Education	38
Books	41
Parents and Guardians	42
Counsel to the Young	45
Advice in relation to Marriage	49
Advice relating to Temporal Affairs	51
Amusements and Recreations	54
On the right occupation of the First Day of the Week	56
War	58
Slavery and Oppression	59
Oaths	60
On Civil Government	61
National Fasts and Rejoicings, and what are termed Holy Days	63
Burials and Mourning Habits	65
Covetousness	66

CHAPTER III. CHRISTIAN DISCIPLINE.

	PAGE.
Introduction. On the Origin of the Christian Discipline established among Friends,	67
Meetings for Discipline,	71
The Yearly Meeting — Its History, Design and Functions,	75
Regulations,	80
Quarterly Meetings,	82
Monthly Meetings,	85
Delinquencies,	90
Ministers,	94
Elders,	97
Memorials,	98
Preparative Meetings,	99
General Advices,	100
Queries,	103
Unanswered Queries,	106
Oversight,	106
Ministers and Elders,	110
Meetings of Ministers and Elders,	111
Queries of the Meetings of Ministers and Elders,	113
Representative Meeting,	115
Care of the Poor,	117
Regulations with regard to Marriage,	119
Records,	123
Removals,	126
Differences and Arbitrations,	127
Appeals,	130
Trust Property,	133
Intoxicating Liquors, Tobacco, &c.,	135
Defamation and Detraction,	136

CHAPTER I.
CHRISTIAN DOCTRINE.

FROM AN EPISTLE ADDRESSED BY GEORGE FOX AND OTHERS, TO THE GOVERNOR OF BARBADOES, 1671.

We do own and believe in God, the only wise, omnipotent, and everlasting God, who is the creator of all things both in heaven and in the earth, and the preserver of all that He hath made; who is God over all, blessed forever; to whom be all honor and glory, dominion, praise, and thanksgiving, both now and forevermore! And we do own and believe in Jesus Christ, his beloved and only begotten Son, in whom He is well pleased; who was conceived by the Holy Ghost, and born of the virgin Mary; in whom we have redemption through his blood, even the forgiveness of sins; who is the express image of the invisible God, the first-born of every creature; by whom were all things created that are in heaven and that are in earth, visible and invisible, whether they be thrones, or dominions, or principalities, or powers; all things were created by Him. And we do own and believe that He was made a sacrifice for sin, who knew no sin, neither was guile found in his mouth; and that He was crucified for us in the flesh, without the gates of Jerusalem; and that He was buried, and rose again the third day by the power of his Father, for our justification; and we do believe that He ascended up into heaven, and now sitteth at the right hand of God. This Jesus, who was the foundation of the holy prophets and apostles, is our foundation;

and we do believe that there is no other foundation to be laid but that which is laid, even Christ Jesus; who, we believe, tasted death for every man, and shed his blood for all men, and is the propitiation for our sins, and not for ours only, but also for the sins of the whole world: according as John the Baptist testified of Him, when he said, "Behold the Lamb of God, which taketh away the sin of the world." John, i. 29. We believe that He alone is our Redeemer and Saviour, even the Captain of our salvation, (who saves us from sin, as well as from hell and the wrath to come, and destroys the devil and his works,) who is the Seed of the woman that bruises the serpent's head; to wit, Christ Jesus, the Alpha and Omega, the first and the last. That He is (as the Scriptures of truth say of Him) our wisdom and righteousness, sanctification and redemption; neither is there salvation in any other, for there is none other name under heaven given among men, whereby we must be saved. It is He alone who is the Shepherd and Bishop of our souls: He it is who is our Prophet, whom Moses long since testified of, saying, "A prophet shall the Lord your God raise up unto you of your brethren, like unto me; him shall ye hear in all things whatsoever he shall say unto you: and it shall come to pass, that every soul which will not hear that prophet shall be destroyed from among the people." Acts, iii. 22, 23. He it is that is now come "and hath given us an understanding, that we may know Him that is true." And He rules in our hearts by his law of love and of life, and makes us free from the law of sin and death. And we have no life but by Him; for He is the quickening spirit, the second Adam, the Lord from heaven, by whose blood we are cleansed, and our consciences sprinkled from dead works, to serve the living God. And He is our mediator, that makes peace and reconciliation between God offended and us offending; He being the

Oath of God, the new covenant of light, life, grace, and peace; the author and finisher of our faith. Now this Lord Jesus Christ, the heavenly man, the Immanuel, God with us, we all own and believe in; Him whom the high priest raged against, and said he had spoken blasphemy; whom the priests and the elders of the Jews took counsel together against, and put to death; the same whom Judas betrayed for thirty pieces of silver, which the priests gave him as a reward for his treason; who also gave large money to the soldiers to broach a horrible lie, namely, that his disciples came and stole Him away by night while they slept. And after He was risen from the dead, the history of the Acts of the Apostles sets forth how the chief priests and elders persecuted the disciples of this Jesus, for preaching Christ and his resurrection. This, we say, is that Lord Jesus Christ, whom we own to be our life and salvation.

And, as concerning the Holy Scriptures, we do believe that they were given forth by the Holy Spirit of God, through the holy men of God, who (as the Scripture itself declares, II Pet. i. 21,) "spake as they were moved by the Holy Ghost." We believe they are to be read, believed, and fulfilled, (He that fulfils them is Christ); and they are "profitable for doctrine, for reproof, for correction, for instruction in righteousness, that the man of God may be perfect, thoroughly furnished unto all good works," II Tim. iii. 16, 17; and are able to make wise "unto salvation, through faith which is in Christ Jesus." We call the Holy Scriptures, as Christ and the apostles called them, and holy men of God called them — the words of God.

We do declare, that we do esteem it a duty incumbent on us to pray with and for, to teach, instruct, and admonish, those in and belonging to our families, for whom an account will be required by Him who comes to judge both quick and dead, at the great day of judgment, when every one shall be rewarded according to the deeds done in the body, whether they be good or whether they be evil; at that day, we say, of the resurrection, both of the good and of the bad, of the just and the unjust, "when the Lord Jesus shall be revealed from heaven with his mighty angels, in flaming fire, taking vengeance on them that know not God, and that obey not the gospel of our Lord Jesus Christ: who shall be punished with everlasting destruction from the presence of the Lord, and from the glory of his power; when He shall come to be glorified in his saints, and to be admired in all them that believe in that day." II Thess. i. 7–10. See also II Pet. iii. 3, &c.

FROM A DECLARATION OF CHRISTIAN DOCTRINE GIVEN FORTH BY THE SOCIETY OF FRIENDS, 1693.

We sincerely profess faith in God by his only begotten Son, Jesus Christ, as being our Light and Life, our only way to the Father, and also our only mediator and advocate with the Father.

That God created all things; He made the worlds, by his Son, Jesus Christ, He being that powerful and living Word of God, by whom all things were made; and that the Father, the Word, and the Holy Spirit, are one, in divine being inseparable; one true, living, and eternal God, blessed forever.

Yet that this Word, or Son of God, in the fulness of time, took flesh, became perfect man according to the flesh, descended and came of the seed of Abraham and David; but was miraculously conceived by the Holy Ghost, and born of the virgin Mary: and also, further declared to be the Son of God, with power, according to the spirit of holiness, by the resurrection from the dead.

That in the Word, or Son of God, was life, and the same life was the light of men; and that He was that true light which enlightens every man coming into the world; and therefore that men are to believe in the light, that they may become the children of the light. Hereby we believe in Christ, the Son of God, as He is the light and life within us; and wherein we must needs have sincere respect and honor to and belief in Christ, as in his own unapproachable and incomprehensible glory and fulness; as He is the fountain of life and light, and giver thereof unto us; Christ, as in Himself, and as in us, being not divided. And that, as man, Christ died for our sins, rose again, and was received up into glory, in the heavens, He having, in his dying for all, been that one great universal offering and sacrifice for peace, atonement, and reconciliation, between God and man; and He is the propitiation, not for our sins only, but for the sins of the whole world.

That Jesus Christ, who sitteth at the right hand of the throne of the Majesty in the heavens, is yet our King, High Priest, and Prophet; in his church, a Minister of the sanctuary, and of the true tabernacle which the Lord pitched, and not man. He is Intercessor and Advocate with the Father in heaven, and there appearing in the presence of God for us, being touched with the feeling of our infirmities, sufferings, and sorrows. And also by his Spirit in our hearts, He maketh intercession according to the will of God, crying, Abba, Father.

That the Gospel of the grace of God should be preached in the name of the Father, Son, and Holy Ghost, being one in power, wisdom, and goodness, and indivisible (or not to be divided) in the great work of man's salvation.

We sincerely confess and believe in Jesus Christ, both as He is true God and perfect man, and that He is the author of our living faith in the power and goodness of God, as manifested in his Son Jesus Christ, and by his own blessed Spirit (or divine unction) revealed in us, whereby we inwardly feel and taste of his goodness, life, and virtue, so as our souls live and prosper by and in Him: and the inward sense of this divine power of Christ, and faith in the same, and the inward experience, are absolutely necessary to make a true, sincere and perfect Christian in spirit and life.

That divine honor and worship is due to the Son of God; and that He is, in true faith, to be prayed unto, and the name of the Lord Jesus Christ called upon, (as the primitive Christians did,) because of the glorious union or oneness of the Father and the Son, and that we cannot acceptably offer up prayers and praises to God, nor receive a gracious answer or blessing from God, but in and through his dear Son.

Concerning the resurrection of the dead, and the great day of judgment yet to come, beyond the grave, or after death, and Christ's coming without us, to judge the quick and the dead; what the Holy Scriptures plainly declare and testify in these matters, we have been always ready to embrace.

1. For the doctrine of the resurrection: "If in this life only we have hope in Christ, we are of all men most miserable." I Cor. xv. 19. We sincerely believe, not only a resurrection in Christ from the fallen, sinful state here, but a rising and ascending into glory with Him hereafter; that when He at last appears, we may appear with Him in glory; Col. iii. 4; I John, iii. 2; but that all the wicked who live in rebellion against the light of grace, and die finally impenitent, shall come forth to the resurrection of condemnation; and that the soul or spirit of every man and woman shall be reserved in its own distinct and proper being, and every seed, yea every soul,

shall have its proper body, as God is pleased to give it. I Cor. xv. A natural body is sown, a spiritual body is raised: that being first which is natural, and afterward that which is spiritual. And though it is said, this corruptible shall put on incorruption, and this mortal shall put on immortality, the change shall be such as will accord with the declaration, "flesh and blood cannot inherit the kingdom of God, neither doth corruption inherit incorruption." I Cor. xv. 50. We shall be raised out of all corruption and corruptibility, out of all mortality; and the children of God and of the resurrection shall be equal to the angels of God in heaven. As celestial bodies do far excel terrestrial, so we expect our spiritual bodies in the resurrection shall far excel what our bodies now are. Howbeit we esteem it very unnecessary to dispute or question how the dead are raised, or with what body they come: but rather submit that to the wisdom and pleasure of Almighty God.

2. For the doctrine of the eternal judgment: God hath committed all judgment unto his Son Jesus Christ; and He is judge both of the quick and the dead, and of the states and ends of all mankind. John, v. 22, 27; Acts, x. 42; II Tim. iv. 1; I Pet. iv. 5.

That there shall be hereafter a great harvest, which is the end of the world, a great day of judgment, and the judgment of that great day, the Holy Scripture is clear. Matt. x. 15; xiii. 39, 40, 41; Jude, 6. "When the Son of Man shall come in his glory, and all the holy angels with him, then shall he sit upon the throne of his glory; and before him shall be gathered all nations," &c. Matt. xxv. 31, 32, to the end, compared with Luke, ix. 26, and I Cor. xv. 52; I Thess. iv. 16, and II Thess. i. 7, 8, to the end; Rev. xx. 12, 13, 14, 15.

These declarations, which are in accordance with the testimony of the approved writings of Friends both ancient and modern, were published in the early days of our religious Society, as setting forth its faith *then*, on these momentous points. They have been officially confirmed and sanctioned by, perhaps, every generation of our members since, and they declare the faith of Friends *now*.

FROM THE LONDON GENERAL EPISTLE, 1736.

And, dear Friends, in order that, as we have received Christ, so we may walk in Him, in all holiness and godliness of conversation, we earnestly exhort that ye hold fast the profession of the faith of our Lord Jesus Christ, without wavering; both in respect to his outward coming in the flesh, his sufferings, death, resurrection, ascension, mediation, and intercession at the right hand of the Father; and to the inward manifestation of his grace and Holy Spirit in our hearts, powerfully working in the soul of man, to the subduing of every evil affection and lust, and to the purifying of our consciences from dead works, to serve the living God; and that, through the virtue and efficacy of this most holy faith, ye may become strong in the Lord, and in the power of his might.

FROM THE TESTIMONY OF THE SOCIETY OF FRIENDS ON THE CONTINENT OF AMERICA.*

The article of belief, which stands foremost in its nature and importance, and that which is the foundation of all others, is the being of one God, — infinite in all His attributes, and existing in His own divine perfections, "from everlasting to everlasting." This one, true, eternal, and incomprehensible God, created and still upholds "all things by the Word of his power." In his infinite goodness, He has been pleased to reveal to mankind a knowledge of *Himself* and of the means of acceptance with Him, so far as, in his wisdom, He saw to be fit, and suited to the condition of the human mind.

From these revelations of the Spirit of God, proceeded the Scriptures of Truth, which were written by "holy men of God" "as they were moved by the Holy Ghost"; and by the operations of the same Spirit, He still influences the hearts of the children of men to practical righteousness, and to a belief in harmonious accordance with the testimony of the Holy Scriptures.

The Society of Friends has declared, both by the concurrent testimony of many of its most eminent members, and in a collective capacity, its firm belief in the Lord Jesus Christ, as the *Saviour* of men; that he was conceived by the Holy Ghost, born of the virgin Mary, — that He wrought miracles in the land of Judea, was hated and rejected by the chief priests and people of the Jews, betrayed by Judas, and crucified under Pontius Pilate; that He rose from the dead the third day, appeared to his disciples, and ascended to heaven, and ever liveth to make intercession for us; that He is now come in Spirit, and hath given us an understanding, being our Prophet and

---

* Issued by a General Committee appointed by the several Yearly Meetings of Friends on the American Continent. Philadelphia, 1830.

High Priest, and head over all things to his church; by whom also God will judge the world in righteousness, whereof he hath given assurance unto all men, in that He hath raised Him from the dead. This we say is that Lord Jesus Christ whom we own to be our life and salvation.

The doctrine of the light of Christ in the hearts of men, taken in connection with the other fundamental doctrines of the Gospel, has been held by the Society from its first being gathered to be a people to the present time. But it ought to be remembered that it is to be carefully distinguished from every other influence which actuates the human mind. Man being endowed with rational faculties, and moreover subject to be operated upon by the prince of the power of the air, the spirit that now rules in the hearts of the children of disobedience, the admonition of the apostle is of peculiar importance: "Believe not every spirit, but try the spirits whether they are of God." I John, iv. 1.

We profess, and firmly believe that this light of Christ in the heart is an unerring guide, and the primary rule of faith and practice; that it is the only medium through which we can truly and livingly attain to the knowledge of God, and the mysteries of the heavenly kingdom.

That the influence of the Holy Spirit must be sensibly experienced, in order to be availing to us, is evident in the very nature of divine things. It is this which produces all heavenly affections and feelings on the obedient mind, which opens the understanding and gives it a right perception, and is in us an operative power, by which we are enabled to resist temptation, and walk in obedience to the law of God. By his powerful operations we are washed and sanctified and justified in the name of the Lord Jesus, for it is "by the Spirit of our God." I Cor. vi. 11. We desire to press the importance of this doctrine, and to guard it against innovations. Nor can a right belief in the Holy Spirit and his influences and operations upon the human mind as the primary source of divine knowledge in us, and the immediate operative power in the work of sanctification and complete redemption, detract from the value of the Holy Scriptures. For as we believe that they certainly proceeded from the same Spirit, so we believe that whatever is contrary to their testimony, in faith or practice, must be a delusion, and in opposition to the immediate influences of the Holy Spirit.

We have ever believed, and as constantly maintained, the truth of that great and mysterious doctrine that "there are three that bear record in heaven, the Father, the Word, and the Holy Ghost, and these Three are One,"—one God, infinite, eternal, and incomprehensible, and blessed forevermore.

The fallen condition of man, as he stands in a state of nature, is a doctrine held forth in the Holy Scriptures, and is of great importance in its application to ourselves, as well as in its intimate connection with the doctrine of redemption by Jesus Christ.

Man was originally created in the divine image. "In the image of God created he him," "crowned him with glory and honor," and set him over the works of his hands. But by transgression he fell from this exalted condition, incurred the penalty of death, and so lost the divine image,—the wisdom, purity, and power in which he was made. This lapse of our prime ancestors not only immediately affected the actual transgressors, but remotely all their posterity. The Society of Friends, in declaring its belief of the extension of the effects of Adam's fall to all his posterity, has been careful to distinguish between those effects, as they apply to us, simply in a state of nature, or as the posterity of Adam in his fallen state, and the *guilt* or *sin* which attaches to us in consequence of our own actual transgression.

In taking a view of the original and present condition of man, at first in the divine image, and afterwards fallen, degenerate, and dead, we are to consider him composed, in part, of an immortal soul, which must eternally exist in a state either of happiness or misery. Thus the doctrine of the resurrection, both of the just and the unjust, of future judgment, of rewards and punishments, and the realities of heaven and hell, is inseparably connected with the belief of the attributes of God, and the immortality of the soul.

And hence the consequence of sin, and of alienation from God, not being confined to the present state of existence, but of eternal duration, the redemption of man becomes one of the most awful, humbling, and exalted subjects which can possibly engage the attention of the human mind. The depth of darkness into which we have been plunged, the awfulness of the consequences attendant on that state, the riches of the love of God, displayed in the redemption by Jesus Christ, and the height of happiness and glory to which we may be raised through that redemption, combine not only to recommend this doctrine to our frequent meditation, but to clothe the mind with the most humbling feelings, and to inspire it with the most animating hopes.

From a careful consideration of the doctrines of the Christian religion, it will be seen that there is an intimate connection of all its parts, and a dependence of the whole on Jesus Christ, in his blessed offices, as the everlasting Foundation. It was on his coming, and what He did for us without us, that the previous forms of devotion were abrogated, and a worship introduced, at once simple and sublime; in which, in humble waiting upon God, we may, as said the apostle, "come boldly to the throne of grace," and hold communion with the Father of mercies, the God of all consolation.

It was He, who, having been crucified, raised from the dead, and exalted by the right hand of God, shed forth the Holy Spirit, by virtue of which both sons and daughters were to prophesy. And those whom He was pleased to call and qualify for the ministry, being ambassadors for Him, boldly declared the necessity of faith in Christ, and of obedience to his divine precepts. And in the exercise of their gifts they were instructed to depend on Him, to be to them mouth and wisdom, tongue and utterance.

By his own regenerating power, He leads the soul through those cleansing operations which were represented by outward baptism, and which consist not in "the putting away of the filth of the flesh, but the answer of a good conscience towards God, *by the resurrection of Jesus Christ.*" I Peter, iii. 21. And in the participation of the divine nature, and through that faith which applies and seals the efficacy of his propitiation, we enjoy the communion of the body and blood of Christ.

He brought life and immortality to light through the gospel, and pointed the minds of the humble believers in Him to a mansion of rest, eternal in the heavens.

He more clearly revealed the relations we hold to God, and to one another, than had been made known under the previous dispensation. The nature of his peaceful reign, and the social virtues characteristic of his kingdom upon earth, which had been set forth before, in the sublime and figurative language of prophecy, He brought down, in his own divine precepts, to the comprehension of the humblest understanding. He commanded us to love our enemies — to do good for evil, and, as a universal rule of action, to do to others as we would they should do unto us. Thus the axe was laid to the very root of the principles of war, retaliation, and revenge, and all the various grades of wrong, oppression, and injustice, among men. And by his Spirit in our hearts, He inspires us with those heavenly affections and feelings, and that universal benevolence, in which man, in every situation, is the friend of man — and, in the prevalence of which, violence no more would be heard in the land, wasting nor destruction within our borders; and a practical illustration would be given of the anthem of the heavenly host; "Glory to God in the highest; and on earth, peace, good will toward men."

OF THE HOLY SCRIPTURES.

We esteem the Holy Scriptures of the Old and New Testament as the authentic testimony of the Spirit, divinely preserved; as the abiding record of the Truth of God; "profitable for doctrine, for reproof, for correction, for instruction in righteousness," and able to make "wise unto salvation, through faith which is in Christ Jesus." As we do therefore believe that these Scriptures were given by inspiration of God, the declarations contained in them rest on the authority of God Himself, and there can be no appeal from them to any other authority whatsoever; that they are the only divinely authorized record of the doctrines which we are bound as Christians to believe, and of the moral principles which are to regulate our actions; that no doctrine which is not contained in them can be required to be believed as an article of faith; and that, whatsoever any say, or do, which is contrary to the Scriptures, though they profess the guidance of the Spirit, it must be accounted a delusion. The great end of the Old Testament Scriptures is to testify of Christ, for "to Him give all the prophets witness:" and we accept the writings of the New Testament, as the record which God hath given us of his Son; and believe that their main purpose is, under the influence of the Holy Spirit, to bring us to the Lord Jesus Christ.

As these inestimable writings were given forth by the Spirit, so a true understanding of the divine will, and spiritual meaning of the application of Holy Scripture, cannot be discerned by the natural, but only by the spiritual man. It is therefore, by the assistance of the Holy Spirit, that they are read with instruction and comfort.

CHAPTER II.

CHRISTIAN PRACTICE.

SECTION 1 — MEETINGS FOR WORSHIP.

The upholding of meetings for the public worship of Almighty God is not only a high privilege, but a solemn duty, for which we are responsible to Him who hath called us; and Friends are affectionately and earnestly advised, duly to attend all our meetings held for that purpose, and not to allow any slight excuse or engagement in their temporal concerns to occasion their absence therefrom, or that of their children or those under their care. And, when assembled, Friends should be diligent in waiting upon the Lord, with fervent desires for the quickening influence of the Holy Spirit, to enlighten the soul to a true sense of its condition; to enable it acceptably to approach the Throne of Grace; to be favored with the enjoyment of his life-giving presence; and to be preserved from wandering thoughts and from a lukewarm and drowsy state. Their deportment should be such as will demonstrate that they are in earnest, in the great duty of waiting upon and worshiping God in spirit. Thus would serious and tender hearted inquirers be encouraged to come and partake, in our solemn assemblies, of that inward and spiritual instruction and refreshment which is, at times, imparted to the souls of such as are humbled before the Lord, and approach his holy presence with reverence and fear.

Let not the smallness of your numbers discourage you

from constantly attending meetings, inasmuch as the words of Christ remain unchangeably true and steadfast, "Where two or three are gathered together in my name, there am I in the midst of them." But, it has been justly observed, that, where remissness and neglect of attending meetings for worship have prevailed, it has often proved an inlet to further declension, and such other liberties as the Truth by no means admits of. Neither let your meetings be neglected because they are sometimes held in silence, for, as you are engaged to wait reverently upon the Lord, 'the hungry seeking for bread, and the thirsty for the water of life, you will receive spiritual refreshment, your strength will be renewed, and you will witness Him to be your sufficient help.

As the constant attendance of meetings for divine worship constitutes an important element in the religious education of our youth, we advise Friends to encourage their children in a seasonable and orderly frequenting, as well of week-day as of first-day meetings; and we would also recommend to those having apprentices or others under their care, to extend kind attention to them, and make such domestic arrangements as may enable them to attend public worship duly and punctually; and when Friends live distant from meetings we would remind them to hold meetings in their families, there to wait upon God, that their hearts may be brought under the awakening, regenerating power of his spirit, that so his blessing may rest upon them.

Seasonable preparation and punctual attendance, at the hour appointed for public worship, are of no small importance. If we hurry away from our outward occupations to the meeting-house, we are in great danger of having our thoughts employed on that in which we have been engaged, and, if late, of interrupting that holy silence which, it is believed, would often prevail if all the members of a meeting were assembled, not only in one place, but at one time, with one and the same great object in view.

And as our religious meetings are to be attended for the worship and honor of Almighty God, wherein we place ourselves more immediately in his presence, may a reverent sense of our responsibility keep us humbly watchful before Him. As this holy care and waiting are maintained a drowsy and listless state will be avoided. Should any be overtaken by drowsiness, we entreat them to seek earnestly by prayer in faith to be preserved from thus dishonoring God and his cause. And if any of our members fall into the practice of sleeping in our meetings, may they be tenderly treated with for their recovery. If they have occupied seats facing the meeting, whether ministers, elders, or others, such are advised to withdraw to a position less conspicuous in the meeting until they are sensible of an overcoming. Where such weakness is apparent in any of our meetings, may all the living members lay it seriously to heart, that a united concern and labor be witnessed therein for the arising of the spring of divine life among them, that so a prevalence of life in the body may preserve all its members from thus bringing reproach upon the name of Christ.

May none yield to the idea that there can be worship in any prescribed system of observances, apart from the ministrations of the Lord's Spirit, or conclude that there can be no true worship, even where the immediate operations of his spirit are enjoyed, without the accompaniment of outward teaching or services. And, when assembled in our religious meetings, may none rest in a vacant stillness or indolent musing, or in thoughts wandering upon earthly things. May all seriously remember that the object of thus assembling is the worship of the infinite, all-seeing, and ever present God, and that it is through the mediation of Him, who died for his people to save them from their sins, and who ever liveth to make intercession for them, without the necessity of any inferior instrumentalities, that the Father is to be approached and reverently worshipped. The Lord Jesus has forever fulfilled and ended the typical and sacrificial worship under the Law, by the offering up of Himself upon the cross, once for all. He has opened the door of access into the inner sanctuary, and appointed spiritual offerings for the service of his temple, suited to the several conditions of all who worship in spirit and in truth. The broken and the contrite heart, the confession of the soul prostrate before God, the prayer of the afflicted when he is overwhelmed, the earnest wrestling of the spirit, the outpouring of humble thanksgiving, the spiritual song and melody of the heart, the simple exercise of faith, the self-denying service of love;—these are among the offerings which He, our merciful and faithful High Priest, is Himself pleased to prepare by his spirit, in the hearts of them that receive Him, and to present with acceptance unto God; these are the essential features of that true worship which stands neither in forms nor in the formal disuse of forms, and may be without words as well as with them, but *must* be in spirit and in truth.

As it hath pleased Divine Goodness clearly to manifest amongst us the way of life and salvation, and to instruct us how to wait for Him, prize, we beseech you, these precious privileges. Keep all your meetings in the power of God, and when thus gathered, be truly concerned to draw near unto Him who will minister to every state and condition, though you may have no outward teaching, and keep you in humble waiting without being restless or uneasy, till it be a proper time to close your meetings. At the close, avoid entering hastily into discourses about the affairs of this life, a practice inconsistent with the Christian gravity, which at such times ought in a special manner to influence the minds of persons so lately assembled for the worship of God.

PRIVATE RETIREMENT AND PRAYER.

We believe that private retirement and prayer is the privilege and indispensable duty of every Christian. It is one of the first engagements of the awakened soul, and becomes the clothing of the minds of those whose lives are regulated by the fear and love of their Creator. In the sacred writings no duty is more clearly set forth. Our Saviour enjoins it upon all his followers by precept, by promise, and by his own blessed example, and we are persuaded that all, who have a just sense of the value of their immortal souls, and of their own sinfulness, helplessness, and dependence, will feel the necessity of looking continually to a higher power, of seeking for better strength, and will thankfully rejoice that they may pray to their Father in Heaven, whose ear is open to their prayers.

We earnestly desire that all may appreciate this high Christian privilege, and with sincere believing hearts and reverential awe, approach the throne of grace, trusting in the mediation of Him through whom we have access by one spirit unto the Father; and, while we know not what we should pray for as we ought, how precious the assurance that the Spirit helpeth our infirmities, and maketh intercession for us according to the will of God.

Let none be discouraged from the performance of this duty by a sense of their transgressions or a feeling of weakness or poverty, but in humility and sincere repentance implore the forgiveness and help of God, who, as they wait patiently before Him will in his own time supply all their need. And if there be any, who, dealing honestly with their own hearts, must acknowledge that they feel no necessity for such prayer, and no remorse of conscience for neglecting it, may these deeply reflect upon the danger of their situation, for such indifference is but the fearful sign of an unhumbled, unrenewed, impenitent heart. While the cause remains the effect will continue; therefore let these beseech God to grant them true repentance through his Holy Spirit, that their indisposition to call upon Him may be removed, and their secret prayers may be accepted and openly rewarded by Him, and the remainder of their lives be so pure and holy that, at the last, they may come to his eternal joy through Jesus Christ our Lord.

Fervent are our desires that we may be indeed a spiritually minded people, and, impressed with the importance to the spiritual life of seasons of retirement before the Lord, we would encourage all, frequently to avail themselves of this privilege. In a well-ordered family many opportunities occur in which the mind may be turned in secret aspirations to the Author of all our blessings, and which often prove seasons of more than transient benefit. We desire that no exception to this practice may be found amongst us. At our Bible-readings, when assembled at our meals, and even when engaged in our temporal affairs, may we cherish that spirit of prayer in which the voice of the Heavenly Shepherd may be distinctly heard, and ability may be received to follow Him, in the obedience of faith, in the path of duty. May the experience of us all be such that we can adopt the words of the Psalmist, " Evening and morning, and at noon, will I pray." How precious the holy settlement, the quiet confidence of those who put their trust in the Lord; and the more we seek for this heavenly abiding, the more fruitful shall we be in that field of offering unto which He may call us, and the more shall we be enabled to glorify our Father in Heaven.

ON READING THE HOLY SCRIPTURES.

Inasmuch as the Holy Scriptures are the means of preserving to us an account of the wonderful dealings of God with his people in ancient time, and especially the prophecies concerning the coming of our Lord Jesus Christ in the flesh, and also plainly set forth his miraculous conception, birth, holy life, blessed example, meritorious death, and his glorious resurrection, ascension, and mediation between God and man, we do tenderly and earnestly advise all our members to be frequent in reading their sacred contents, and meditating thereon, in a humble reliance upon the Holy Spirit which gave them forth. And we exhort parents and heads of families to seek that ability from God which alone can enable them to instruct their children and families in the doctrines and precepts of the Christian religion, as contained in the Bible.

And, dear friends, encourage a frequent and diligent reading of the Scriptures in your families, for in them are contained the promises of salvation and of eternal life. The possession of these inestimable writings is a precious privilege, for which we must give account. May the reading of them in our families ever be conducted with reverence, and with minds gathered under the teachings of the Holy Spirit. Let not the period of silent waiting, on these occasions, be so short as to exclude or interrupt inward retirement and prayer. And we would encourage Friends so to dwell under spiritual exercise, on account of the children and other members of their household, that the word of tender counsel, or encouragement, or the offering of prayer, or thanksgiving, seasoned with grace, may not be withheld.

In addition to the practice of the daily reading of the Holy Scriptures in your families, be encouraged, dear friends, often to read them in private. Cherish a humble and sincere desire to receive them in their genuine import. Ask of God that your meditations upon the sacred writings may be under the influence of the Holy Spirit. The Comforter alone can open the understanding to the Truth as it is in Jesus. And, while we fully acknowledge that these Scriptures are given by inspiration of God, let us ever bear in mind that it is only "through faith which is in Christ Jesus," that they "are able to make wise unto salvation." As this precious faith is sought for, and prevails, the evidence of the Spirit of God in our hearts confirms our belief in the divine authority of these inestimable writings, and increases our gratitude for the knowledge of that redemption which comes by the Lord Jesus, of whom they so largely testify.

ON GIFTS AND SERVICES FOR THE RELIGIOUS BENEFIT OF OTHERS.

We rejoice with thankfulness in the Christian concern evinced by the members of our religious society, and in all rightly directed efforts made by them, for the social, moral, and religious improvement of our fellow-men, and desire to encourage them, individually, to faithfulness in occupying the talent received, "as they that must give account," in dependence upon his grace, and in loving service to Him who loved them and gave himself for them.

Whilst careful to uphold the gospel standard in the things of God, we desire to be preserved from limiting in any degree the fullness and the freeness of the operation of the Holy Spirit. We thankfully acknowledge the goodness of the Lord in the diversities of gifts, intellectual as well as spiritual, which in his care for the church he is pleased to confer upon its several members.

Believing that the Lord has some service for every

member of his church, Monthly and Preparative meetings are recommended, to lend their aid, as way may open, to the promotion of Scripture schools, Mission schools, and other associations for spreading the knowledge of the Gospel, for the instruction of the ignorant, for the reformation of the vicious, and for the relief of the sick, the poor, and the distressed; and to encourage all our members, particularly our young men and women, to labor faithfully for the good of those around them, in accordance with the special gifts with which they may be intrusted, and in simple obedience to the guiding of the Holy Spirit.

When differences occur, Friends are encouraged to be prompt in undertaking, and prudent in exercising the blessed office of peacemaker. The patient endeavors of faithful friends in this service will doubtless be crowned with success, in proportion as their own minds are seeking to the Lord Jesus, for assistance in performing an office, on which He has pronounced his blessing, and in endeavoring to lead the minds of contending persons to a sense of the absolute necessity for all true disciples to live in peace, one with another, and to forgive one another, even as God, for Christ's sake, has forgiven them.

We would especially and earnestly encourage all who are engaged in the important service of instructing the young in the Holy Scriptures, or in their mutual study to edification, to seek by earnest prayer for the help of the Holy Spirit, to enable them to do all to his glory, and for the conversion of souls to Christ.

Faithful Friends should feel it necessary, and an imperative duty, early to visit, in the love of God, young convinced and well inclined persons, for their encouragement, help, and furtherance in the truth.

In the exercise of our various gifts, may there be a constant advancement from strength to strength, and may zeal for that which is good be ever tempered with heavenly wisdom. Let nothing take the place of that love which draws the soul to Christ as its rest and home. May all keep the eye single unto Him, with subjected hearts, prepared to receive every fresh manifestation of his counsel. The services of his household are various, but to each member of it the language is applicable: "Be ye clean that bear the vessels of the Lord." The work of the Lord is ever an humbling work, bringing low and keeping low. Many are its conflicts and humiliations, but unspeakable are its joys. "Where I am," saith our Holy Redeemer, "there shall also my servant be;" "If any man serve me, him will my Father honor."

May we ever bear in mind our Saviour's declaration: "Without me ye can do nothing." Great, then, is the necessity of believing in and waiting for the qualification and the prompting of His Spirit to move and guide us in all our attempts at service for the good of others; whether in the circle of our own religious society, as those of the minister, the elder, the overseer, the committee intrusted with duties in the church, or the member of the body who speaks to the matter before the church, or in that large "field" which "is the world." How carefully should each one wait on Him, that they may neither withhold that which is required, nor move without his requiring. "When He, the Spirit of Truth, is come, He will guide you into all truth."

And, dear friends, whatever may be the duration of our earthly existence, no life is too long for the performance of the duties which He who measures it out, appoints for it. Beware, then, we entreat you, of the beguilements of ease and self-indulgence; of being absorbed by the cares of the world or hindered by its entanglements. Dwell in retirement of spirit before the Lord, and in the habitual exercise of the faith and love of Christ. Whether it be in the family, the social circle, the place of business, or more prominently before the public, let the light of the gospel, and the evidence that you have been with Christ, shine through all. The parent, the man of business, the citizen, each has a testimony to bear for Christ. Let our prayers be fervent, in the name of Jesus, for ourselves and for others. May those upon whom it rightly devolves be diligent in feeding the Lord's flock; and may none, whatever their position, overlook the lesser openings for duty. A word of counsel, of reproof, or of encouragement, spoken in season, in ever so broken a manner, in the family and social circle, or more publicly, how good it is! How often does it reach the witness in the hearts of others! How often does the blessing of the Lord attend it! Let us bear in mind the Christian duty of watching over one another for good. Each may be called to manifest his interest by word or deed on behalf of some brother, or sister, and thus to follow in the footsteps of our Divine Master, whose whole life was marked by sympathy for the sorrows and infirmities of man.

ON SIMPLICITY, MODERATION, AND SELF-DENIAL.

How impressive are the words of our Holy Redeemer, in which he describes his true followers. "They are not of the world, even as I am not of the world." He is the Immanuel, elect and precious, the image of Him who is invisible, in whom the righteousness and grace of God are revealed to man. And it is the high privilege of his disciples to follow his steps, to be conformed to his holy image; to be like Him, pure, and separated in spirit from the world, meek and lowly in heart, not seeking to gratify self, but in all things given up to spend and be spent for the good of others, to do or to suffer according to the will of God. This is the path which our Divine Master hath Himself marked out and consecrated for us — a path of self-denial, humility, and holiness. Let none therefore deceive themselves by any means. The lust of the flesh, the lust of the eye, and the pride of life, are not of the Father, but are of the world; and, whether it be in our personal habits or attire, in our style of living, in the general tone of our conversation or reading, in the mode of our spending our time or our money, in the character of our occupation, or in the manner of conducting our outward affairs; whether it be in that we do or in that which we leave undone, all that in anywise fosters the desires of the flesh, or of the vain and unregenerate mind, impairs the health and vigor of the Christian life. In looking at the holy example of his Lord, the humble believer is made deeply sensible that much yet remains for him to attain. But, as he advances on his course, he will be more and more constrained by the love of Christ to follow after Him in simplicity and godly sincerity, often faint, yet still pressing forward. The standard is a high one, but it is set before us in infinite wisdom and love, by Him who is willing to supply all our need.

How important, in its connection with the great work of the Holy Spirit, is the duty of cultivating a tender religious susceptibility! Christianity is intended to influence the whole life and conversation. Some of its most precious promises relate to the daily conduct and experience of the believer. "I will dwell in them and walk in them," saith the Lord. Marvellous condescension! Blessed is he, who, in the living sense of it, abides continually in the filial fear of offending God. His tastes and affections being renewed from above, he will separate himself from that which the Lord hateth and which his Spirit reproves. Faithfulness to the Divine requirings in the details of life, leads him into nonconformity with the world; and in this nonconformity he is of necessity a marked man amongst the worldly or less restrained. It was a deep consciousness of the practical character of true religion, which led our forefathers to be distinguished from others. Often and feelingly did they declare that they affected no singularity and imposed no merely human restraints; that they had no pleasure in offending their neighbors, and no stoical indifference to personal suffering, but that it was in the exercise of a good conscience towards God and man, that they were constrained to differ from others in these respects. Like them, we would plead for conformity unto Christ. The testimony which we receive from Him is to simplicity, truth-speaking, and self-denial. These we continue to esteem to be among the distinguishing features of complete practical Christianity, and by them we trust that our members may ever desire to be known.

And, forasmuch as a true Christian practice, and every branch of it, is the fruit and effect of the inward sanctification of the heart by the Spirit of Christ, for which we are required frequently to wait on Him in all humility and lowliness of mind, we tenderly advise that everything tending to obstruct or divert the minds of children, or those of more advanced years may be carefully avoided and taken out of the way. And, it being evident that the glory and vanity of the world and the pleasures and diversions of it are of this nature and tendency, we advise that all our members be good examples to their children and those about them, in a humble and circumspect walking, and with all plainness of habit and speech; and also that they be very careful not to indulge their children in the use and practice of things contrary thereto.

"It is required in stewards that a man be found faithful." Happy is that man who, seeking to maintain a good conscience towards God, hath ceased to live unto himself, and is living unto Him who died for us and rose again.

Those who desire that they may be helped to glorify God in their body, and in their spirit, which are God's, will be brought to feel that this is not the place of their rest; their hearts being set on heavenly treasure, that which is earthly and perishable will have less place in their affections; their moderation — the right and temperate use of the Lord's outward gifts — will appear unto all men; it will be their concern to be kept from the love of ease, from undue creaturely indulgences, and from the luxuries of life. Regulated by this Christian standard, our personal expenditure, our style of living, the furniture of our houses, the supply of our tables, the plainness and simplicity of our apparel, the right use of our leisure time and of our property, will evince, so far as these things are concerned, that the love of the world is losing its hold upon us, and that the love of Christ is growing stronger within us.

LOVE AND UNITY.

PART I.

"God is love." He is omnipresent. His love extends to all, both saint and sinner. "God so loved the world that He gave his only begotten Son, that whosoever believeth on Him might not perish." And the Son so loved the world that he gave Himself for the sins of the world,— the just for the unjust. And the Holy Spirit, who is one with the Father and the Son, and the agency whereby the grace, or "favor and assistance of God" hath appeared, He so loves the world that He saith, "come." And the Church, which is the Bride, the Lamb's wife, so loves the world that she saith, "come." And the response must be, and is, from every true and living Christian, "come;" and this because he loves the whole world, the sinner as well as the saint. For "if any man have not the spirit (consequently love) of Christ he is none of His."

This love is broader than unity, because the disciple, the friend of Christ, may and must love even the enemies of Christ. Yet he can have unity only with the friends of Christ,—with such as are engrafted into the same vine, and partake of the same spirit; and their unity stands not in oneness of idea, but in oneness of Spirit,—in that oneness which Christ prayed the Father that his disciples might experience; "that they may be one in us." And although gospel love be more extensive and broader than Christian unity, yet the unity of the spirit, which is not dependent upon oneness of idea, is broad enough to embrace the whole "household of faith," including all true believers, branches of the True Vine, wherever found, in every denomination, in every kindred, tongue, and people. And this gospel love, now so largely and sweetly augmented by the unity of the spirit, is yet further enhanced, though its boundaries be narrowed, by oneness of idea or unity of belief, and blessed are they who maintain and enjoy this love and unity in the "bond of peace."

It is a precious truth to us in our fallen condition, "that God was in Christ, reconciling the world unto Himself, not imputing their trespasses unto them." Christ, who knew no sin, who was a propitiatory offering for our sins, and for the sins of all mankind, who enlighteneth every man that cometh into the world, and who is ever present with his people, as "their Teacher to instruct them, their Counsellor to direct them, their Shepherd to feed them, their Bishop to oversee them, and their Prophet to open divine mysteries to them,"* was the foundation of our forefathers, and this foundation is ours.

* George Fox's Journal.

It was to this experimental knowledge of Christ, that our early predecessors were engaged to gather all men, that they might really be prepared, sanctified, and made fit temples for Him to dwell in. By one spirit they were baptized into one body; and, rooted and grounded in love, they were, through the help of their Lord, united one to another in upholding an open and decided testimony to the gospel in its primitive purity.

"Let brotherly love continue." It is the token that we are the children of God, who is emphatically Love. It is the evidence that we belong to Christ. The psalmist compares the unity of the brethren to the anointing oil and the fertilizing dew. Where it is wanting there is no true fragrance nor fruitfulness in the church. May the Lord, Himself, cause this fragrance and this fruitfulness to abound yet more and more amongst you, to his praise.

PART II.

Among the gospel precepts, we find nothing more strongly and frequently recommended by our Lord Jesus Christ and his apostles to the primitive laborers, than that they should love one another; and, as we are sensible that nothing will more contribute to the peace and prosperity of the church, than a due regard to this advice, so we earnestly desire that it may be the care and concern of all Friends to dwell therein, and in the unity of the spirit to maintain love, concord, and peace, in and among all the churches of Christ.

Seeing our comfort as a people depends upon our care to maintain peace and fellowship amongst brethren, in all our services, we earnestly recommend an humble and condescending frame of spirit unto all; that with godly fear, wisdom, and meekness, we may be ordered in all our respective services; that every high and rough thing may be laid low; that all occasions of striving may be prevented, and the peace of the church of Christ preserved and increased amongst us.

Whilst it is at all times the duty of members of the church faithfully to maintain the truth, and whilst some of them may rightly feel themselves called upon openly to oppose error, we believe that there is hardly anything more inimical to the growth of vital religion, than indulgence in the spirit of religious controversy. Satan triumphs when he can make the name of Jesus a word of strife and debate among the professed followers of the Lord. Let us, therefore, each of us mind our own calling by keeping our eye single to the Lord; and then shall we know that "the fruit of the spirit" will, in the sight of others, be " in all goodness, righteousness and truth," and to ourselves joy and peace; that so every one may come to seek peace and pursue it, and none be apt to take offence, but each in his own particular, be more careful to rectify his own failings and imperfections, than curious in observing, censuring, and exaggerating those of others. This will lead to the exercise of mutual forbearance and forgiveness, one of another, by which the occasions of contention will be avoided, and the church will be preserved in a state of peace and tranquillity. "Follow peace with all men, and holiness, without which no man shall see the Lord; looking diligently lest any man fail of the grace of God; lest any root of bitterness springing up trouble you, and thereby many be defiled."

LIBERALITY AND BENEVOLENCE.

"Blessed is he that considereth the poor." It is our desire that we may all of us be kept in that state of watchfulness from day to day, and in that sense of our responsibility to God, in which we may be enabled to ascertain whether a due portion of our time, our sympathies, and our substance, is devoted to the great duty of visiting the poor in our respective neighborhoods, to the inspection of their condition, and to the relief of their wants; and we wish to appeal to our dear young people to consider whether a larger portion of their time, the means they may have at their disposal, and that which they could spare from the superfluities of life, might not be acceptably devoted to this object. It is important to ourselves, as well as to those who are in need, that the due support of institutions, whose object is the relief of human suffering, should not be substituted for the personal visiting of the poor in their own habitations, and the administering to their wants. We would warn those that are rich in this world, that they apply not the blessings of God to the indulging of their appetites in pleasure and vanity; but that they be ready to do good, and to contribute to the relief of those who are in necessity. The principal, if not the only satisfaction, a man of a truly Christian disposition can have, in the possession of affluence and the increase of the things of this world, must arise from the greater opportunities put into his hands of doing good therewith.

We fear that some of our members are indulging in habits of expense in attire, furniture, and manner of living, which are not only inconsistent with the simplicity of the Gospel, but a constant call for much of that property, which would be better employed in feeding the hungry, and of that time, which might be occupied in visiting and cheering the habitations of human misery. "The trimming of the *vain* world," said our worthy elder William Penn, "would clothe the *naked* one." It is not, however, with such only that we plead on behalf of the indigent.

We wish those who in appearance and manner are generally consistent with our self-denying profession, to be clear that a due proportion of their time and substance is spent in the relief of distress. The degraded and demoralized state of the poor, in many places, and the great prevalence of crime, are deeply to be deplored. We therefore entreat Friends in their respective situations, in town and country, to search out the causes of these evils and to encourage their neighbors, and unite with them, in their efforts to apply a remedy. And, seeing it is sin which separates the soul from communion with God, and that ignorance, intemperance, vice, and irreligion so much prevail, may our sympathies be awakened for such of our fellow creatures as are suffering from these causes, with an earnest endeavor that, under the blessing of God, we may be made instrumental in effecting a real improvement in the domestic, moral, and religious state of these our fellowmen.

ADVICE IN RELATION TO THE MINISTRY.

A living, rightly authorized ministry, has ever been a blessing to the Church. It is the prerogative of Christ Jesus, our Lord, to choose and to put forth his own ministers. A clear apprehension of Scripture doctrine, or a heart enlarged in love to others, are not of themselves sufficient for this work. Whatever may be the talents or scriptural knowledge of any, unless there be a distinct call to the ministry, the Society of Friends cannot acknowledge it, and, except there be a sense of the renewed putting forth and quickening influence of the Holy Spirit, we believe it to be utterly unsafe to move in this office. Our blessed Lord, just before his ascension, commanded his disciples to wait at Jerusalem until they were endued with power from on high, knowing their inability, without that power, to speak in his name, for the conversion of the nations. It was this power that enabled them to speak boldly in the name of Jesus, this alone that made them able ministers of Christ, whose preaching was not with enticing words of man's wisdom, but in demonstration of the spirit and of power.

The Spirit of God, being the foundation of all true knowledge and experience, both in ministers and in hearers, we earnestly exhort that all should reverently and diligently wait upon and mind it. Ministers, in their public services especially, ought always to attend closely to their several and peculiar gifts, and minister the word faithfully, as it is manifested and revealed to them, observing a modest behavior in the exercise thereof, and a care, on no occasion, to exceed the measure of their gifts.

We earnestly caution and entreat all such among you as find themselves concerned in Christian love to exhort and admonish others, that they be especially careful of their own conduct; that by circumspect walking, in all holiness of life and conversation, they may be living examples of the purity and excellence of the advice they recommend. Looking into the state of this part of our Society, the necessity that such be examples in their daily walk appears exceedingly great, particularly in a diligent attendance of all our meetings for worship and discipline; therein to be very deep and weighty in spirit, laboring, with an ardor of soul suited to the occasion, for the arising of the ancient spring of life, which of a truth is the crown of our assemblies, and the ground of our joy and rejoicing in Christ, and one in another.

Ministers should be frequent in reading, and diligent in meditating upon the Holy Scriptures, and be careful not to misquote, misconstrue, or misapply them. In preaching, writing, or conversing about the things of God, let them keep to the use of sound words or scripture terms. They are advised to be cautious of laying undue stress on their testimony, by too positively asserting a divine motion, and frequently repeating the same, as the baptizing power of truth, accompanying the words, is the best evidence of the gift, in all true gospel ministry.

Ministers should be guarded when led into disputed points of doctrine in their testimony, not to make objections which they do not clearly answer, nor give repeated expectations of coming to a close of their remarks. And they are advised to guard against unnecessary preambles and repetitions; against hurting meetings by unnecessary additions towards their conclusion; against all unbecoming tones, sounds, and gestures; and against all affectation. They should carefully avoid presuming to prophesy in their own spirits against any nation, city, town, people, or person; or delivering prophetic declarations of any kind, without the most clear and certain evidence of divine authority.

As it is one of the duties especially incumbent on elders to be helpful to those engaged in the ministry, a trust which they cannot properly discharge without the aid of that wisdom which is from above, there should be such a prevalence of love between the ministers and elders, that the ministers may feel that they have a kind and sympathizing friend in every elder. Where this mutual love and confidence are maintained, they are not only a strength to each other, but are encouraging examples to the church. We also advise ministers to have it very much at heart, to maintain a perfect harmony and good understanding with the monthly meetings to which they belong; that as the said meetings may sometimes find themselves concerned to advise ministers respecting their conduct in meetings, or otherwise, they show themselves ready to hear and receive advice, as well as to teach and instruct.

We do in much love caution those who are concerned in the work of the ministry, to watch over their own spirits, and not to be hasty or censorious in passing judgment respecting the state of those who hear them, but to manifest that, in the exercise of their ministry, they are led by the love of God, and that their aim is to be instrumental in administering spiritual consolation and strength to the churches where they may come.

Ministers and elders should be very careful, whilst they are engaged in necessary business, not to become entangled with the cares of the world, and should guard against an inordinate desire of accumulating wealth, that thus they may be examples of Christian moderation and contentment in all things; and let them be careful not to overcharge themselves with trade or other outward engagements, to the hindrance of their service for truth, or engage in employments of which they have neither knowledge nor experience, but pursue such business as they are acquainted with.

We tenderly advise all who travel in the work of the ministry, that they not only shut their ears against all private information, tending to the defamation of persons or families, and to stir up disputes and contentions in meetings for discipline; but that they rebuke and reprove the person or persons who shall attempt to prejudice their minds with any private information of that nature; and we further advise them, while so travelling, to be very prudent in their conduct, not as busy bodies, nor meddling with family or personal affairs in which they are not concerned, or required to assist, that they be careful not to make their visits burdensome or the gospel chargeable, and, as soon as their service in the ministry is over, that they return to their habitations, and there take a reasonable and prudent care of their own business, households, and families.

Ministering friends should be careful not to hurt one another's service in public meetings, but let every one have a tender regard for others; that nothing be offered with a view to popularity, but in humility and the fear of the Lord.

When ministers are favored with a clear intimation that it is required of them to speak to the people, it is advised that they attend to it seasonably, not deferring it until the meeting becomes too weary to be benefited thereby.

And lastly, as prayer and thanksgiving are an important part of worship, let them be offered in spirit and in truth, with a right understanding, qualified by grace. When engaged herein, ministers should avoid many words and repetitions, and be cautious of too often repeating the high and holy name of God or his attributes, or of passing from supplication into declaration, as though the Lord had need of information.

EDUCATION.

Education, in the most comprehensive sense of the word, constitutes an important part of Christian discipline.

It has long been the concern of this Society and often expressed, that our children and youth may be brought up in the "nurture and admonition of the Lord," in a love of virtue, and in a strict regard for truth and integrity — and that you, dear friends, who fill the important station of parents, may set that example of an humble Christian life, which so beautifully enforces the pure principles of the gospel. The moral, intellectual, and spiritual condition which prevails in the family, determines more than any other influence in childhood, the character of its individual members.

The education of our children in schools and academies, has always been an object of care and solicitude in the Society of Friends, and its institutions of learning have received the prayerful attention of its most devoted members, from an early period of its history; and, at this later day, when the world around us has made such great progress in the general diffusion of knowledge, we trust that Friends will continue to hold an honorable position among their fellow professors in the church universal, as active promoters of sound, liberal, and useful education; and, to that end, it is earnestly desired that they may be increasingly impressed with the importance of providing, within our own Society, the advantages afforded by schools, colleges, and other higher institutions of learning, which are enjoyed by those who are not in profession with us.

We may be well assured that the most exalted piety is consistent with the highest attainments in learning, and that truth in science is not in conflict with the faith which we profess, but a perpetual testimony to its truth and verity; and that intellectual discipline tends to the enlargement of the understanding, and thereby extends the field of individual usefulness. The powers of the mind were given to be cultivated to the fullest extent, in the fear of the Lord, both for the happiness of their possessor and for the advantage of his fellow-men.

The well educated is no less likely than the ignorant man to be an humble follower of Christ, and, when his powers are consecrated to the service of his Lord, he can bring all his gifts as tithes into the storehouse. All truth is from the same Divine Source. Minds rightly tempered by religious experience, and in harmony with the mind of God, are peculiarly fitted to investigate the paths of science, and to cultivate the fields of literature and art. The cultivation of the mind not only prepares for more efficient service under the direction of the Holy Spirit, but it conduces, also, to that wide toleration and charity, which are essential to the preservation of Christian love and unity.

We would therefore earnestly advise that Friends make liberal provision, and at personal sacrifice, if need be, for the intellectual training of their children, under circumstances favorable to their moral preservation and spiritual growth, and that they cherish that generous disposition towards teachers, which will encourage well qualified persons to engage in this responsible work, — not only those who are able to instruct in the different branches of learning, but who are also concerned to cooperate with the Society, in its religious endeavors to excite a love of virtue, and to show out of a good conversation an example consistent with our principles.

A care should also be exercised, in the choice of school books, to select such as are healthy in their moral tone. We are also religiously concerned that our young people, while receiving that education which will fit them for usefulness, may be trained up in the knowledge of the Holy Scriptures. They should be made acquainted in very early life with the instructive narratives and leading facts of the Old Testament, with the types and prophecies which represented beforehand the coming and the character of Christ, and especially with that message of love and mercy to fallen man, which is contained in the Gospel. May it also be impressed upon their tender minds, that the same Holy Spirit, which revealed the Divine truths of the Bible to holy men of old, doth in this day, by its perceptible influence, illuminate those truths, and reveal to the understanding of the humble disciple the saving knowledge thereof.

We esteem it of great importance, that children and youth be led to examine for themselves the external evidences of the Christian religion, and that their attention be directed to those parts of Scripture which elucidate our particular doctrines and testimonies. Thus, as they advance in life, they will know on what grounds their profession rests, and be able to give to others an intelligent reason for the hope which they entertain.

While we observe with satisfaction the increasing interest manifested by Friends in First-day schools for scriptural instruction; and are fully assured that this service is owned and blessed of the Lord, we desire to caution Friends not to rely too much on this work, and so to neglect the moral and religious instruction of their children, either in their families or in schools for secular education.

Friends who have the prosperity of Truth at heart, should take care, if suitable opportunities and occasions offer, that their children be taught the modern languages, so that, when they are grown up, as it shall please the Lord to dispose and incline them, they may be of service therein to the church. Instances have not been wanting in the earlier and later history of this Society, when such gifts and acquirements have been sanctified, in some of our own members, and they have thereby become serviceable instruments in their Master's hand.

BOOKS.

Books may be regarded as companions, which insensibly infuse somewhat of their spirit and character into those who converse with them. It behooves us to exercise a sound discretion as to what publications we admit into our houses; that neither we nor our children may be hurt by that reading which would have a direct, or even a remote tendency to leaven our minds into the spirit of the world, and to unfit us for the sober duties of life. The books which we introduce to the young require careful selection; they may give a bias to the mind, and materially influence the future character. Some, we fear, find access to our families, which are calculated to give false views of real life, and to lower that standard of morals which Christianity upholds; and others, though they may not stimulate evil passions, are adapted to lessen the attachment of our youth to the principles of their education, or even to rob them of the tenderness of their consciences, and alienate them, it may be, by slow gradations, from the fear of God.

We therefore earnestly exhort all parents, heads of families, and guardians of minors, that they not only abstain from such reading themselves, but that they prevent, as much as in them lies, their children, and others under their care and tuition, from having or reading books and papers tending to weaken their confidence in the Christian religion, or to create the least doubt concerning the authenticity of the Holy Scriptures, or of those saving truths declared in them, or such as malign our religious Society, or distort or misrepresent its principles, lest their minds should be poisoned thereby, and a foundation be laid for great evils. And it is earnestly recommended to all members of our religious Society, that they discourage and suppress the reading of pernicious novels, plays, and other bad books. And printers and booksellers, in profession with us, are cautioned against printing, selling, or otherwise circulating such books.

PARENTS AND GUARDIANS.

Parents, heads of families, and all who have the care of the young, are earnestly entreated that you diligently lay to heart your work and calling for the Lord, and the charge committed to you, not only in being good examples to the young, but also that you use your power in your own families, in educating your children and wards in modesty, sobriety, and the fear of God; and that you frequently put in practice the calling together of your children and households, to wait upon the Lord in your families; that, receiving wisdom and counsel from Him, you may be enabled seasonably to exhort and encourage them to walk in the way of the Lord; to be diligent in reading the Holy Scriptures, and in observing the duties and precepts of holy living therein recommended; admonishing them to keep to that plainness and simplicity in apparel, speech, and behavior, which the Spirit of Truth leads into, and which becomes the humble, self-denying followers of Jesus; and may you also encourage them in the constant attendance of meetings for public worship.

In the earlier periods of life, much of the care of children rests upon mothers. To them the precious infant is committed, with the implied charge on behalf of its Heavenly Parent, — "Take this child and nurse it for Me," — and we desire that in all cases their pious endeavors may be strengthened by the co-operation of the fathers. The youthful mind is very soon susceptible of serious impressions, and we believe that if parents are careful to watch the most favorable opportunities, they may instil religious truths, lay a foundation for correct principles, and give a right bias to the affections, which may be greatly blessed at a future day. The safe ground on which parents can proceed is, so to live and so to wait before the Throne of Grace, as to be enabled to pour forth their earnest prayers for the blessing of the Most High.

How solemn are the responsibilities thus involved, and how needful that the parental obligations should not be put aside nor turned away from, under any feeling of discouragement or want of qualification! It is not on the highly gifted parent alone that the duty is imposed of training up his children in the fear of God, and in the knowledge of the Holy Scriptures; it is a charge laid upon every parent; and the sense of our own insufficiency, however deeply felt, will prove no valid plea for neglect, when we are called to account for the trust committed to our keeping. Let none, whilst endeavoring, with single minded earnestness and in reliance upon higher aid, to discharge this duty, doubt that ability will be granted to them; let them rather believe that they will reap the reward of their efforts in a blessing upon their children and upon themselves. The endearing relation which subsists between parents and their offspring, ought surely to awaken in the hearts of the former, earnest breathings of spirit, that they may be helped to train their children, even from very early years, in tenderness of conscience, in obedience to the restraints and guidance of the Holy Spirit, and in the love of Christ our Saviour.

We affectionately exhort all who have the care of children and young persons, constantly to bear in remembrance the great value of a tender conscience; and to turn their attention to the secret instructions of Divine Grace, reproving for evil, and bringing peace for doing well. Be concerned, dear friends of this class, that the wills of those intrusted to your charge, become subjected to the Divine will in early life; encourage them to fix their affections on things which are eternal; set before them the necessity of being converted from the evil of their own hearts, and kept clean from the sin which abounds in the world; impress them with a sense of the holiness and purity of God, and of His righteous Law; instruct them in the invaluable truths of the Bible, and lead them to seek after the practical application of its precepts and doctrines, under the influence of the Holy Spirit.

Friends, in every situation in life, are advised to take due care to bring up their children in some useful and necessary employments, that they may not spend their precious time in idleness, which is of evil example and tends much to their hurt; and not to suffer their substance to be bestowed upon them, to furnish such things as tend to pride, and to lift them up in vanity, or affect them with the vain fashions of the world.

COUNSEL TO THE YOUNG.

For you, dear young friends, the objects of our sympathy and love, we would express our strong desire, our fervent prayer, that the ever-watchful care of the Heavenly Shepherd may be over you for good. Yours is a period of life beset with many and strong temptations. Even in the most favored allotment there are snares both secretly and more openly laid for your feet. Oh that we could prevail with you all to come unto Christ, to confide in him as your Saviour, and to take his yoke upon you.

If happily your hearts have been made tender before the Lord, and you know what it is for the hand of God to be upon you, be careful that you never resist the working of his power; be frequent in presenting yourselves before the Lord; commune with your own hearts; do not wait too long for miraculous impressions of duty, but watch for the gentlest intimations of the Holy Spirit; and, in whatever acts of dedication He may call for the acknowledgment of your love and allegiance, give yourselves up to his service with a willing and a ready mind. Think on the blessing pronounced upon the pure in heart; ask of God that He will keep you from evil thoughts and wrong imaginations, that in your intercourse with the world and one with another, in your words and all your conversation, you may be blameless and harmless.

Give a portion of each day to reading and meditating upon the sacred volume in private, steadily directing your minds to Him who alone can open and apply the Scriptures to our spiritual benefit. In these seasons of retirement, enter into a close examination of the state of your own hearts, and, as you may be enabled, pray to the Almighty for preservation from the temptations with which you are encompassed. And here we would especially commend to you the duty and the real necessity of prayer. Be not discouraged at the coldness which you may find, and lament in your own hearts. The warm glow of devotion is not at our own control, but God, who looks into the heart, will see there the real desire to love Him and to serve Him, and as we persevere, we believe our Father in Heaven will mercifully help our weakness, and grant us the warming influence of his grace.

Be very careful, we beseech you, not to read publications of an irreligious or immoral tendency, or which openly or indirectly inculcate views which would, in the least degree, weaken your faith in the mysterious but sacred and all-important doctrines of that salvation which is in Christ. Feeling your own weakness, and the limited powers of the human intellect, may you accept these doctrines in reverence of soul, in simplicity, and in godly sincerity. Pray that you may be kept in that humble, dependent state of mind in which the Lord, by his Spirit, often gradually unfolds the deep things of his kingdom, and grants a holy faith in the experience of their reality.

Let not pleasure, profit, or advancement in life, however allowable these may be, take the *first* place in your desires, but guard in an especial manner against the first sacrifices of duty to inclination. If you check improper or wrong desires in their infancy, your victory over future temptations will be the more easy, and through faith in Him that hath loved us, and hath overcome, you will in time be more than conquerors; but, if you shrink from the conflict, or resign the victory to the tempter, you will be despoiled of the armor designed to preserve you in future assaults; each effort will be more and more difficult, and it may be that you will unhappily feel yourselves unable to resist, in your further progress through life, temptations which, in the fresh morning of your day, you would have held in abhorrence. Cherish carefully, as a priceless treasure, this youthful tenderness of conscience.

We earnestly desire that you may all not only be professors with us, but, by obedience to the spirit of Christ, become real possessors of the truth as it is in Jesus. We are persuaded that in the eyes of many amongst you, the cause of religion has indeed appeared lovely. Why, then, is there not a full surrender to its power and to its convictions? "The Lord loveth an early sacrifice." A sacrifice of what? Nothing, be assured, that will not in the end prove hurtful to your best interests. We fear that the difficulties of entering upon a religious life have been magnified. Many a susceptible young heart, touched with a sense of the Saviour's love, feels drawn towards Him, but fears lest if it once yield itself up to Him, some great sacrifice will be required that it will not be enabled to make; some painful effort, it knows not what, that there will be no strength to meet. But these anxieties are groundless. "Fear not!" "It is your Father's good pleasure to give you the kingdom." And if such be his gracious design, can you not believe that He will himself kindly and gently lead you in the way to the kingdom? His promise is sure, — "They that seek me early shall find me." His service is a service of love. He has himself declared, "My yoke is easy, and my burden is light." He stands at the door of every heart, knocking for admittance. Oh, that none of you may be so unwise as to keep Him out by indifference or lukewarmness, or by too engrossing a love of the things of this life, forgetting the Giver in the enjoyment of his numberless gifts, but that you may open your hearts unreservedly to the gentle influences of his pure spirit. Trust in Him with simple, childlike faith, and then you will know of the blessedness and peace there is in serving Him, and of finding your own wills to be not only in subjection to, but in harmony with the Divine will. Then "hard things will be made easy and bitter things sweet," and in the hour of trial and temptation you will know that you have a friend on whom you can rely with confidence and safety, "Who was in all points tempted like as we are, yet without sin," and who knows and can help us in all our sorrows and weaknesses, "for in that He himself hath suffered, being tempted, He is able to succor them that are tempted."

We tenderly sympathize with those of you who feel that you are, as it were, passing through the wilderness, and whose souls are often discouraged because of the way. To the young disciple, the conflict is at times severe. Temptation is strong, whilst the heart is weak; tremblingly halting between Christ and the world. In straits such as these, may you never yield to the suggestions of the tempter. Consult not how far you may safely indulge yourselves, or how nearly you may approximate to the ways and habits of the world. Be in earnest to realize a yet closer and more dependent walk with God. The faith that leads you unto Christ will, as it is exercised, give you the victory through Him. May you more and more feel that you are not your own; that you are bought with a price. Where much is given, there, in the great day of final account, will much be required. May all your talents be freely offered unto the Lord, and consecrated to his blessed service. There, you will find true liberty, and abundant scope for the right employment of every talent, and in the enjoyment of his love your cup will overflow with blessing and praise. We desire that as you grow in Christian experience and attainment, you will gladly and cheerfully exercise all those gifts which it may please the

Lord in his mercy to bestow upon you, to your own comfort, to the help of the church, to the relief and uplifting of suffering humanity, and to the praise of his great and worthy name. The prize is before you; it is a prize not of earth, but of heaven; not a corruptible crown, but an incorruptible. It is to be obtained not without effort, but through the exercise of faith, hope, and love. Remember that to her who loved much, much was forgiven. Press on towards this prize, we entreat you. Shrink not from the warfare; so shall the crown immortal be yours; so shall you forever rejoice in God, your Saviour, and adore his abundant mercy who hath prepared for those that love Him "an inheritance, incorruptible, undefiled, and that fadeth not away."

ADVICE IN RELATION TO MARRIAGE.

Marriage, being a Divine ordinance, and closely connected with the temporal and spiritual condition of man, we earnestly desire that in the choice of companions for life, all may seek unto the Lord for his guidance; not allowing any mere exterior advantages to be the primary motive in this engagement; ever bearing in mind that an accordance in religious principles is essential to the perfectness of such a union.

Parents are advised to exercise a religious care in watching over their children, and to endeavor to guard them against improper connections in marriage; and that they be joined with persons of religious inclinations, suitable dispositions, and diligence in their business. It is particularly recommended to all parents, to endeavor to cultivate such habits of confidence, and freedom in the truth, with their children, as may render it easy for them early to consult their parents, on a subject of such importance.

And, seeing that the real enjoyment of life is far more effectually secured by contentment, with simple habits, than by an appearance or mode of living which entails anxiety, or risk, we would strongly advise parents, whilst they exercise a prudent care over the interests of their children, not to be unduly anxious to secure worldly advantages for them, on entering the marriage state. We would also affectionately encourage our younger members, when looking towards this most important step, to be satisfied to set out in life, in a manner befitting their circumstances, instead of seeking to imitate, in their style of living, the example of those who possess larger resources. They would, thus, on the one hand, avoid the necessity of unduly deferring their union, and, on the other, be less exposed to the temptation of launching into business beyond their means.

We desire that the solemnization of marriage may in all cases be conducted in the fear of the Lord, and in humble dependence on his blessing, and that in the details of these highly interesting occasions, our principles with regard to display be observed; and, while the proceedings of the marriage day may naturally be characterized by cheerful enjoyment, that those concerned may never pass the boundary line of Christian simplicity and moderation.

It is further advised, that, after parents and guardians have suffered their children to engage one another's affections, they do not break off such engagement upon any mere worldly account, and that they wait upon and seek the Lord for their children, in proposals of marriage, before they give any encouragement thereunto.

We strongly recommend Friends to avoid and discountenance very early proceedings in regard to marriage, after the death of husband or wife; regarding such conduct as tending to the dishonor and reproach of our Christian profession.

ADVICE RELATING TO TEMPORAL AFFAIRS.

Let friends and brethren, in their respective meetings, watch over one another in the love of God and with Christian care; particularly admonishing that none trade beyond their ability to manage honorably; that they use few words in their dealings; and keep their word in all things, lest they bring, through their forwardness, dishonor to the precious truth of God.

It is advised, that the payment of just debts be not delayed beyond the time promised and agreed upon; nor occasion of complaint be given to those who are dealt with, by backwardness of payment, when no time is limited.

And we advise and counsel all Friends, for their own good, that they keep to such lawful and honest employments, for a necessary support of themselves and their families, as they well understand and are able to manage; and that they be very careful to avoid all inordinate pursuit after the things of this world, by such ways and means as depend too much upon the uncertain probabilities of hazardous enterprises; but that they rather labor to content themselves with such a plain way of living, as is most agreeable to the self-denying principle of truth which we profess, and which is most conducive to that tranquillity of mind that is requisite to a religious conduct.

We would caution every individual against imprudently entering into joint securities with others; and earnestly desire that Friends keep strictly on their guard, that none, through any specious pretences of rendering acts of friendship to any, with safety to themselves, may risk their own peace and reputation, and the security of their families, by disregarding the salutary advice of the wise man, "Be not thou one of them that strike hands, or of them that are sureties for debts."

It is earnestly recommended, that Friends frequently inspect the state of their affairs, and promptly settle their accounts; and, when any find themselves unable to pay their just debts, or have not more than sufficient to pay them, that they immediately disclose their circumstances to the overseers or other judicious Friends, and to their principal creditors, and take their advice how to act; and be particularly careful not to pay one creditor in preference to another.

If any fall short of paying their just debts, and an arrangement be made with their creditors, to accept a part instead of the whole, notwithstanding the parties may look upon themselves as legally discharged of any obligation to pay the remainder, yet the principle of universal righteousness enjoins full satisfaction to be made, if ever the debtors are able to do it. And, in order that such may the better retrieve their circumstances, we exhort them to adopt a manner of living in every respect the most conducive to this purpose.

Those who, whilst honestly and diligently endeavoring to provide for their families, have to encounter many difficulties, have a strong claim on the sympathy of their Friends; yet they need not fear, as they continue to place their whole trust in our Heavenly Father, but that He will care for them in such way as He sees meet. But if any, whether of the more affluent, or of those who cannot be ranked in this class, are deviating from safe and regular methods of business, if they are carried away by uncertain and hazardous, though plausible, schemes for getting rich, if they yield to a desire rapidly to enlarge their possessions — such are in imminent danger. They cannot justly expect the blessing of the Most High on such pursuits; their spiritual eye becomes dim; and they do not perceive with clearness that light which would enable them to perfect holiness in the fear of God.

We would tenderly advise those who may have acquired a competency of outward substance, to watch the proper period at which they may withdraw from the cares of business, and when disengaged from the regular concerns of trade, or other occupations, to beware how they employ their property in investments which may involve them anew in care and anxiety. We affectionately desire that neither these nor other cares may disqualify them from acting the part of faithful stewards, in the employment of their time, their talents, and their substance; or, from being concerned, above all things, through watchfulness unto prayer, to have their lamps trimmed and oil in their vessels, that, when the solemn close of life shall come, they may, through redeeming love and mercy, be prepared to enter into the joy of their Lord.

Our brethren who are employed in the various active pursuits of life claim our sympathy. Those engaged in trade, especially, are at times exposed to close competition, and to the temptation to pursue their own interest in a way inconsistent with true justice in dealing. They may be much tried by the small profits often resulting from a course of honest industry and diligent attention to business; but it should never be forgotten that there is a sterling integrity which the christian should always maintain; that there is a standard set before him in the New Testament which he should always keep in view.

Knowing how suddenly many are removed by death, it is recommended that care be taken that Friends who have estates to dispose of, by will or otherwise, be advised to make their wills in time of health and strength of judgment; to prevent the inconveniences, loss, and trouble, that may fall upon their relations and friends, through their dying intestate. Making such wills in due time, can shorten no man's days, but the omission or delay thereof has proved very injurious to many.

It is recommended that Friends who have young children do designate in their wills faithful Friends to be their guardians. It is also advised that, in making their wills, they have a strict regard to justice and equity, and be not actuated by caprice or prejudice, to the injury of those who may from their kindred and near connection, have a reasonable expectation; nor (although occasion may have been given or taken) carry any resentment to the end of life; remembering that we all stand in need of mercy and forgiveness.

Friends are earnestly recommended to employ persons of competent legal ability and of good repute, to write their wills; as great inconvenience and loss, and sometimes the pecuniary ruin of families, have happened through the unskillfulness of some who have taken upon them to prepare wills. And all Friends who may become executors or administrators are advised to proceed without unnecessary delay, to take all the legal measures which the duties and obligations they have assumed may require.

AMUSEMENTS AND RECREATIONS.

Parents, and all others, upon whom the training of children devolves, should be careful to provide such attractive employment, and means of healthful and innocent recreation, for the leisure hours of those under their charge, in the intervals of study and other daily duties, as become rational and immortal beings, accountable to the Great Giver for the employment of every moment of time, and such as shall, by making home more attractive, remove from them, as far as possible, any temptation to indulge in the popular, and too frequently injurious amusements and diversions of the day. There are recreations, in the enjoyment of rural life and scenery, in the society of well chosen associates, in examining the works of creation, and in the pursuits of literature, science, and natural history, which are full of interest, and tend to improve the mental and moral faculties; and there are occupations for the young, in relieving the distressed and in caring in many ways for the neglected and destitute, which encourage their sympathies, enlarge their Christian interests, and prepare them for future usefulness in the church and in the world.

As our time passeth swiftly away, and our delight ought to be in the law of the Lord; it is advised that a watchful care be exercised over our youth, to prevent their going to stage-plays, horse-races, entertainments of music and dancing, or any such vain sports and pastimes, and being concerned in lotteries, wagering, or other species of gaming.

It is our conviction, that as the mind is renewed by Divine grace, all these vain amusements will seem inconsistent with the restraints of the gospel, and incompatible with that quietness and peace of mind which are the portion of the watchful christian. The life of the christian is not a dull and cheerless existence,—there are no joys here below, to be compared with those of the renewed soul, in the faithful service of the Lord. As the heart becomes truly given up to the love of Christ, the services of pure and undefiled religion, the improvement of the mind, and the varied duties which we owe to our fellow-men, will be found abundantly sufficient to employ the energies of the soul; while the sweet consolations of the Holy Spirit will give far truer and more abiding refreshment than any mere gratification of taste or sense can afford. It is not, then, for the diminution, but for the increase of their happiness, that we would affectionately invite our dear friends to submit all their pursuits, even those which may be intended as recreations, to the restraints and government of the Holy Spirit. As this is the case, the various duties and enjoyments of the present life will be placed in their true relation to the life to come. The occupation of our leisure hours, and, with many, these make up a large amount in the sum of their responsibilities, our associations, our reading, all our varied engagements of a social or more public nature, will be baptized into the Christian spirit.

To look upon this life as the training-school for heaven, is at once the christian's duty and consolation. The sense of his responsibilities and dangers is too strong to allow him to court temptation. He has no time to squander upon trifles. His renewed tastes have no relish for vain or frivolous pursuits. He asks not how near he can approach, without danger, to the gaieties and amusements of the world, but rather seeks to know how closely he can follow that Saviour, by whom the world is crucified unto him and he unto the world.

ON THE RIGHT OCCUPATION OF THE FIRST DAY OF THE WEEK.

We believe, from the evidence of Holy Scripture, that it is a duty enjoined upon man by his Creator, to observe one day in seven as a day of rest, to be especially devoted to religious purposes. We therefore regard it as incumbent on us, to assemble together on the first day of the week, for the public worship of our Father in Heaven, and for an open acknowledgment of our allegiance to Him. This we believe to be in accordance with the practice of the apostles and early christians, who met together on this day in the name of their risen Lord; and we esteem it no small privilege to live in a community where this religious duty is recognized. And, while the remembrance of our Creator, and of our obligation to Him, should at all times be present with us, it is our concern that the day more particularly devoted to public worship may be rightly observed.

May we also seriously examine, whether the mode of spending that portion of the day, not occupied with the attendance of our religious meetings, is such as is likely to contribute to the eternal interests of the soul; or whether the character of our pursuits, and even of our conversation, is not such as shall tend to dissipate any religious impressions which we may have received. Many have derived great increase of spiritual strength, both on this and on other days, from private devotional retirement, from reading the lives and experience of the Lord's faithful servants, and from reading the Holy Scriptures, with minds turned to their Divine Author, in desire that He would bless them to their comfort and edification.

We earnestly recommend to Friends, on this day of the week, to assemble their households for the reading of the Scriptures and for waiting upon the Lord, — a practice to which we wish particularly to call the attention of those who live in remote and secluded situations. And to all Friends, who, either as parents or guardians, are intrusted with the training of children and youth, we would urge that a portion of the day be devoted to their instruction in the Holy Scriptures; and especially, that these should become familiar with the account of the life and teachings of our Lord Jesus Christ, upon earth; and that such seek for ability to teach them the way of salvation by Him, as recorded in the Scriptures.

And we desire the encouragement of those of our members who may be drawn, in the constraining love of the gospel, to engage in the responsible work of Scriptural instruction, either in First-day schools among ourselves, or in mission schools on this day among the poorer and less favored classes; and may such prayerfully seek for opportunities to enter upon these services in simple dependence on the Divine blessing.

WAR.

As it hath pleased the Lord, by the breaking forth of the glorious light of the Gospel, and the shedding abroad of his Holy Spirit, to gather us to be a people, to his praise, and to unite us in love, not only one unto another, but to the whole creation of God, by subjecting us to the government of his Son, our Lord and Saviour, Jesus Christ, the Prince of Peace, it behooveth us to hold forth the ensign of the Lamb of God, and, by our patience and peaceable behavior, to show that we walk in obedience to the example and precepts of our Lord and Master, who hath commanded us to love our enemies, and to do good to them even that hate us. Wherefore, we entreat all who profess themselves members of our Society, to be faithful to that ancient testimony, borne by us ever since we were a people, against bearing arms and fighting; that, by a conduct agreeable to our profession, we may demonstrate ourselves to be real followers of the Messiah, the peaceable Saviour, of the increase of whose government and peace, there shall be no end.

This Christian and truly scriptural testimony against all war, is as precious to us as ever it was. We dare not believe that our Lord and Saviour, in enjoining the love of enemies and the forgiving of injuries, has prescribed a series of precepts which are incapable of being carried into practice; or of which the practice is to be postponed till all shall be persuaded to act upon them. We cannot doubt that they are incumbent upon the Christian now; and that we have, in the prophetic scriptures, the distinct intimation of their direct application, not only to individuals, but to nations also.

We recommend that our members, consistently with our ancient and uniform testimony, refuse the payment of all taxes, expressly or specially for the support of war, whether called for in money, provisions, or otherwise. We also advise that Friends carefully avoid censuring or judging each other, in respect to the payment or non-payment of any mixed taxes, or such as a part thereof goes to the support of war, and a part for civil government.

SLAVERY AND OPPRESSION.

Notwithstanding the legal forms of Slavery in this nation have been abolished, the spirit of oppression remains, and the rights of the neglected and down-trodden still call for the guardian care of the philanthropist and the Christian. We would therefore encourage our members to bear them and their wrongs upon their hearts, and endeavor to improve every providential opening to do them good, remembering the language of Him who has watched over and done so much for us,—"Inasmuch as ye have done it unto one of the least of these, my brethren, ye have done it unto Me."

The testimony which the Society of Friends has so long borne against the iniquitous system of slavery, has, we humbly trust, been blessed of our Heavenly Father, and we believe it right to record our thankfulness that our Holy Head led us in this way. May we be encouraged to follow more closely the guidance of His Spirit, embracing every right opening for service, in promoting the abolition of slavery and the slave trade, in those countries where unhappily it still exists, and also in healing the wounds, and abating the injuries, which this iniquitous system has produced, wherever it has prevailed, removing, as far as may be, the ignorance, immorality, and helplessness, which have followed in its train.

We desire that the aborigines of our country may continue to receive, not only the sympathy, but the Christian efforts of Friends, to secure and maintain their rights, both civil and social. May all our efforts for the help and improvement of the oppressed and unfortunate everywhere, be based upon the conviction that they are not only members of the great brotherhood of mankind, but are, alike with us, the objects of the love and mercy of our common Father, and heirs of the promise of salvation and eternal life.

OATHS.

Our Christian testimony should be faithfully maintained against the burthen and imposition of oaths, according to the express prohibition of Christ, "Ye have heard that it hath been said by them of old time, thou shalt not forswear thyself, but shalt perform unto the Lord thine oaths; but I say unto you, swear not at all; neither by heaven, for it is God's throne; nor by the earth, for it is his footstool; neither by Jerusalem, for it is the city of the great King; neither shalt thou swear by thy head, because thou canst not make one hair white or black; but let your communication be yea, yea; nay, nay; for whatsoever is more than these cometh of evil." "But," says the apostle, "above all things, my brethren, swear not; neither by heaven, neither by the earth, neither by any other oath; but let your yea, be yea; and your nay, nay; lest ye fall into condemnation." Believing therefore as we do, that no argument can invalidate a prohibition thus clear and positive, we are bound religiously to regard it; and whilst we feel gratitude for the continuance of that indulgence, by which our affirmation is accepted, let us evince our sincerity in relation to this testimony, by faithfully maintaining it.

We entreat, that, when any Friend has occasion to make an affirmation, he be very considerate, and sure of the truth of what he is about to affirm, remembering that the command, "Thou shalt not bear false witness," is as binding as "Thou shalt not swear;" and as well in the gospel as in the law. Also, that the stretching forth the hand in token of appeal to the Most High before the magistrate, forms no part of an affirmation, but of *an oath*.* If a due sense of the obligation to truth-speaking adequately rests upon the mind, its effect will be manifest, even in the deportment of those who are giving evidence.

ON CIVIL GOVERNMENT.

It is our principle, and hath ever been our practice, to be subject, either by doing or suffering, to whatsoever government is set over us. We have ever maintained that it is our duty to obey all the enactments of civil government, except those which interfere with our allegiance to God. We owe much to its blessings; through it we enjoy liberty and protection, in connection with law and order; and, whilst bound by our sense of religious conviction not to comply with those requisitions which violate our Christian principles, we desire ever to be found of those who are

---

* We desire that our members should understand that no magistrate has authority to bid a Friend to hold up his hand in administering an affirmation, and considering the real difference between an oath and an affirmation, that no Friend can consistently do so.

quiet in the land; a condition favorable to true Christian patriotism, and in which, services valuable and useful may be rendered to the community.

Liberty of conscience being the common right of all men, and particularly essential to the well being of religious societies, we hold it to be incumbent upon us to maintain it inviolably among ourselves; and therefore exhort all in profession with us, to decline the acceptance of any office or station in civil government, the duties of which are inconsistent with our religious principles, or, in the exercise of which, they may be under the necessity of exacting of their brethren any compliances against which we are conscientiously scrupulous.

Believing that we are called to show forth to the world, in life and practice, the blessed reign of the Prince of Peace, we cannot consistently join with such as form combinations of a hostile nature against any; much less in opposition to those placed in authority; nor can we unite with or encourage such as revile or asperse them, for it is written, "Thou shalt not speak evil of the ruler of thy people." Acts, xxiii. 5.

In fulfilling the duties of life, when occasions occur in which we may consistently serve the community in a civil capacity, let us be concerned to know whether it is right for us to be thus engaged; and be watchful that such undertakings do not mar the work of the Lord in our hearts, or interfere with our line of service in his church. The like watchfulness should be maintained, when taking a public part with others in associations for the purpose of lessening the mass of vice and misery which may prevail around us, or in works of more extended philanthropy.

NATIONAL FASTS AND REJOICINGS, AND WHAT ARE TERMED HOLY DAYS.

Believing as we do in the spirituality and freedom of the gospel, and that the worship and prayers which God accepts are such only as are produced by the influence and assistance of the Holy Spirit, we cannot consistently unite with any in the observance of public fasts, feasts, and what are termed holy days, when such forms are devised by man's will for Divine worship.

In accordance with our Christian testimony against war, we refrain from the custom of illuminating our houses, or performing any act as a token of joy for victories obtained. And we believe all occasions of public rejoicing frequently lead to practices inconsistent with that meek and quiet spirit which should clothe the disciple of Jesus, and prove an inlet to excesses which estrange the mind from God. It is not in this way that we should manifest our gratitude for national blessings, but by endeavoring, through redeeming love and power, to live more and more in the spirit of the gospel, and thus to hold out an example of genuine Christian conduct, remembering that righteousness alone exalteth a nation.

We believe that at times the Lord is pleased, in an especial manner, to visit nations by his judgments, and that they call for deep humiliation before Him, and for that repentance which includes a real turning away from all our evil works. This was the great feature of that memorable fast which obtained the divine favor for Nineveh, after the prophet had been sent to pronounce its destruction. The true and acceptable fast to the Lord was declared by the prophet Isaiah to be, not the bowing of the head for a day, but the right performance of acts of justice and mercy. How loudly then are we, as Christians, called upon to beware of depending upon any temporary or external performances, and to observe that daily and continual fast, which consists in the obedient homage of the soul to its Almighty Creator and Redeemer!

The believers in Christ are spoken of as a royal priesthood. Under the new covenant, we are all invited to the great privilege of offering "spiritual sacrifices, acceptable to God, by Jesus Christ." As we come to enjoy this privilege, we are brought not to depend one upon another, or upon stated performances in the public worship of God, and are confirmed in the truth, that typical rites and ceremonies are no part of the scriptural dispensation under which we live.

In supporting these our views of the liberty of the gospel, let us be careful to prove, by our conduct and conversation, that we walk in the fear of God, who rules in the kingdoms of men, and are engaged to serve Him and worship Him in spirit and in truth. And, while true to our own convictions, let us not needlessly wound the feelings of others, whose views, conscientiously held, lead them into observances with which we cannot consistently unite. May we cherish that true love of our country which would lead us frequently to the Throne of Grace on its behalf, that so, whilst we cannot lift up the sword in its defence, our prayers and intercessions may ascend availingly to Him, in whose hand is the prosperity of nations.

The names in ordinary use of the days of the week, and of most of the months, are of idolatrous origin, and repugnant to the Christian testimony borne by faithful Friends, for the sake of which they patiently endured many revilings. Let not the reproach therefore of singularity turn any aside from denominating the months and days according to the numerical mode of expression, or from bearing a faithful testimony against these, and all other forms of idolatry and superstition.

BURIALS AND MOURNING HABITS.

Our members are affectionately cautioned against the practice of wearing mourning apparel, on the occasion of the decease of relations and friends. It tends to occupy the thoughts with useless and frivolous subjects, at a time when it is peculiarly important, that nothing should interfere with those precious visitations of the love of God to the soul, which often in an especial manner accompany the afflictive dispensations of the Most High, in the death of our near connections, contriting the heart, and comforting the true mourner. The custom not unfrequently imposes a straightening burthen on families, which they are little able to sustain, and is, moreover, in many instances, a token of sorrow not really felt; and this includes a departure from that strict truthfulness, which, in deed as well as in word, ought ever to mark the Christian character.

Friends are advised to avoid all extravagant expenses about the interment of the dead; and to bear a sound Christian testimony against the erection of monuments in Friends' burial grounds, as well as against all inscriptions of a eulogistic character, over the graves of deceased Friends. Nevertheless, we consider it to be no violation of such testimony, to place over or beside a grave a plain stone, to be of the dimensions established by this Yearly Meeting in 1852, viz., not to exceed fifteen inches in height above the surface of the ground; the inscription on which is confined to a simple record of the name, age, and date of the decease, of the individual interred.

Burials of persons not members of our religious society, may take place in our burial grounds, provided they be in all respects conducted as the burial of Friends are conducted. Friends will exercise discretion as to complying with any application that may be made in such cases, and as to appointing a meeting for worship on the occasion.

In order that burials be commendably and decently accomplished, and our testimonies maintained, as well as for the assistance of those immediately concerned, monthly meetings are advised to appoint a committee to attend thereat, and also to see that all burial grounds are properly enclosed and kept.

COVETOUSNESS.

As our Lord and Saviour Jesus Christ exhorted and warned to take heed and beware of covetousness, (which is idolatry,) we are concerned that all our members may guard against pride, over-reaching, defrauding, and hastening to be rich in the world, which are pernicious and growing evils. Let them be watched against, resisted, and suppressed, in the fear and dread of Almighty God, and have no place or countenance among us; remembering the admonition of the apostle Paul: "They that will be rich, fall into temptation and a snare, and into many foolish and hurtful lusts, which drown men in destruction and perdition. For the love of money is the root of all evil; which, while some coveted after, they have erred from the faith, and pierced themselves through with many sorrows." Beware therefore, dearly beloved, lest you, also, being led aside by the love of this world and the deceitfulness of riches, fall from your own steadfastness.

CHAPTER III.

CHRISTIAN DISCIPLINE.

INTRODUCTION — ON THE ORIGIN OF THE CHRISTIAN DISCIPLINE ESTABLISHED AMONG FRIENDS.

The plan of discipline in the Society of Friends, so wisely laid down for them by their predecessors, has been maintained for nearly two centuries without material alteration. This plan is characterized by that simplicity on the one hand, and that precision on the other, which, under Providence, could alone insure its usefulness and stability.

While we cannot doubt that, in its construction, George Fox and his coadjutors were favored with the gracious aid of the Holy Spirit, it is also evident that their attention was closely fixed upon the pattern of discipline presented to them in the New Testament. Their system was, indeed, more developed than that of the primitive believers is known to have been, especially as it regards the subordination of one class of meetings to another; but, with regard to main principles, as well as in many distinct particulars, the views and practices of Friends, with respect to church order, appear to be the same as those of the primitive Christians.

The acknowledgment of Christ as the only Head and priest of his people; the direct dependence upon Him, as the present ruler of the church; the divine origin of the gift of the ministry and the absence of all human restriction, as to the person who might exercise it; the voluntary support of the poor; the appointment in every monthly meeting, of officers to manage the funds raised for that purpose, and of elders and overseers to watch over the flock of Christ, — all being distinct, in their official characters, from the prophets or preachers, — the settlement of disputes, not before the magistrates of the land, but by the arbitration of brethren; the private admonition of offenders as the first step in discipline; the select conferences of preachers and elders; the making of rules, the choosing of officers, the disownment and restoration of offenders, by the assembled believers; are points which distinguish the simple religious polity of the earliest Christians; and all these points are steadily maintained in the Society of Friends.

There are two points connected with our view of church-government which are worthy of special notice. The first is, the absence of all ecclesiastical domination, or of any distinction between a priesthood in power, and a laity in subjection. No such distinction appears to have been known among the immediate followers of Christ, or in the first and purest age of the churches which they planted, and none such exists among ourselves. Our views on this point are, indeed, by no means opposed to the just influence of the more experienced members of the church, or to the proper authority of appointed overseers; but we consider ourselves to be brethren possessed of equal privileges; and we conceive it to be the duty of the church to conduct its own affairs, and to govern itself. And here there is no place, on the part of individuals, for a personal independence, or impatience of restraint: because, as far as Christian discipline extends, every member is controlled and governed by the body at large.

Now, it is very obvious, that such a form of church-government can be safe and salutary, only while we maintain a still higher principle — that of the supremacy and perpetual superintendence of Christ himself. This is a doctrine in which Friends have at all times believed. Often have they been led to call to mind the words of the prophet: "Unto us a child is born, unto us a son is given: and the government shall be upon his shoulder." Isaiah, ix. 6. Often have they found occasion to recur to the doctrine of the apostle, that God hath put "all things" under the feet of Jesus, and given "Him to be the Head over all things to the church." Eph. i. 22.

What, then, is the agency by which Christ conducts his reign, and orders the affairs of his universal people? Scripture and experience alike declare that it is the agency of the Holy Spirit. It is by his Spirit that He brings his children into subjection to his will, qualifies them for their respective offices in the body, and guides them, individually and collectively, in their course of duty.

The second subject alluded to is, the belief of Friends, that a manifestation of the Spirit is given to every man to profit withal; and that the living members of the church, in their endeavors to promote the religious welfare of others, will not fail to receive, as they humbly seek it, his gracious aid and guidance. Whether, in such endeavors, we act as private individuals, or in the official character of overseers of the flock, it is still in dependence on our Divine Master, and in obedience to the government of his Spirit, that our duties ought to be performed. We believe that it is thus, and thus only, that we can with confidence offer up the prayer of the Psalmist; "Establish thou the work of our hands upon us; yea, the work of our hands establish thou it." Ps. xc. 17.

But further — when christians meet in their collective capacity, for the purpose of regulating the affairs of the church, and of promoting the cause of religion, Christ is their rightful President. And, it is our firm belief, that, as they reverently wait upon Him, they will find Him present to assist their deliberations, to prompt their efforts, and to direct their decisions. That such was the happy experience of the primitive believers, may be shown from the Scriptures; and there is surely no good reason why christians, in the present day, did they fully rely on God, should not enjoy the same blessed privilege.

We, therefore, consider it to be our duty to conduct all our meetings for discipline, with immediate reference to the government of Christ, and to the guidance of the Holy Spirit. Whether we are engaged in appointing officers; in acknowledging ministers; in deliberating upon their prospects of service; in admitting members; in dealing with delinquents; in extending advice to subordinate meetings; or in discussing propositions made with a view to the welfare of the body; — whatever subject, indeed, connected with religion and morality may occupy our attention, — we believe it to be right, humbly to wait for Divine direction, and to yield to that judgment, on the subject before us, which appears to be most consistent with the mind of Christ.

Believing that, of every question which can arise in the church, there must be a right conclusion, and in the further belief that, as they diligently seek his counsel, Christ will lead his dependent followers into that conclusion, we admit in our meetings for discipline, of no division of members — of no settlement of any point by majority. The Clerk gathers and records the judgment of the meeting, and it is his duty, during the course of every discussion, to take care that proper order be preserved. But he has no personal authority over the assembly, no power to put any subject to the vote, and no casting vote of his own.

That this is a principle worthy of our Christian profession, and eminently conducive to the welfare of the church, cannot be denied; and, although its full effect may often be prevented by the infirmity of our nature, we are bound to acknowledge that it has worked well in practice; and it continues to be the case, that questions are never settled in our meetings for discipline — monthly, quarterly, or yearly — by a division of the members. Have we not, then, much cause for thankfulness to Him who is Head over all things to the church, that He still condescends to preserve us, as a people, in some degree of practical dependence on his own authority; that He still brings us, from time to time, into the same judgment; that He still enables us, when our opinions differ, to condescend one to another in love?

Certain it is, that the more we are weaned from the eagerness of the carnal mind, and brought to wait patiently on the Lord, the better we shall be prepared to receive and follow his counsel; the more eminently we shall enjoy the unity of the Spirit in the bond of peace.

MEETINGS FOR DISCIPLINE.

Early after the establishment of meetings for worship, those for discipline were instituted; and, as the right maintenance of these is indispensable to the welfare of the society, Friends are entreated to be diligent in the attendance of them, and to encourage the attendance of their families.

By the term discipline, is to be understood all those arrangements and regulations which are instituted for the civil and religious benefit of a christian church. The meetings for discipline are, of course, for the purpose of carrying those objects into effect. Their design was said by George Fox to be, the promotion of charity and piety. He mentions in his journal, that some meetings for discipline were settled in the north of England in 1653. The earliest meetings of this character, of which we have any account, in this country, were established in 1658.

Christianity has ever been a powerful, active, and beneficent principle. Those who truly receive it, no more "live unto themselves;" and this feature and fruit of genuine Christianity was strikingly exhibited in the conduct of the early Friends. No sooner were a few persons connected together in the new bond of religious fellowship, than they were engaged to admonish, encourage, and, in spiritual as well as temporal matters, to watch over and help one another in love. Each member was at liberty to exercise the gift bestowed upon him, in that beautiful harmony and subjection which belong to the several parts of a living body, from the analogy to which the apostle Paul draws so striking a description of the true church: "Ye are the body of Christ, and members in particular."

It was one of the earliest features of our religious economy, to elevate the character of women by recognizing them as helpers in spiritual as well as in temporal things; holding in the former, as in the latter, a distinct place, and having duties which more peculiarly devolved on them. For this purpose, meetings were established among them with a special regard to the care and edification of their own sex. The views of George Fox in regard to the establishment of these meetings are conveyed in the following passages: "Faithful women, called to a belief of the truth, and made partakers of the same precious faith, and heirs of the same everlasting gospel of life and salvation as the men are, might in like manner come into the profession and practice of the gospel order, and therein be meet-helps to the men, in the service of truth and the affairs in the church, as they are outwardly in civil and temporal things; that so all the family of God, women as well as men, might know, possess, and perform, their offices and services in the house of God; whereby the poor might be better taken care of; the younger sort instructed, informed and taught in the way of God; the disorderly reproved and admonished, in the fear of the Lord; the clearness of persons proposing marriage more closely and strictly inquired into, in the wisdom of God; and all the members of the spiritual body, the church, might watch over and be helpful to each other in love."

And in order for the regular and easy proceeding in the service and discipline of the church, coordinate meetings of each sex have been, by Divine assistance, set up and established, serviceable and subordinate one unto another; as *Preparative*, consisting of Friends belonging to one or more particular meetings for worship; *Monthly*, consisting of as many preparatives as may most usefully compose the same; *Quarterly*, to consist of as many monthly meetings as are thought useful to constitute the same, to meet together once in three months; *Yearly*, consisting of all the quarterly meetings in New England, east of the Connecticut river, having the general care and oversight of all the meetings within its limits, to meet annually on Rhode Island. No quarterly meeting can be set up, divided into two, or discontinued, but by the Yearly Meeting; no monthly meeting, but by the quarterly meeting; no preparative meeting, or meeting of worship, but by the monthly meeting, which is the lowest meeting that has the right of disowning members. These meetings are subordinate and accountable, thus: the preparative to the monthly, the monthly to the quarterly, and the quarterly to the yearly meeting; so that, if at any time, either of these bodies be dissatisfied with the proceedings of any subordinate meeting within its limits, such subordinate meeting, when required thereto, ought, with readiness and meekness, to render a satisfactory account accordingly. Although the men's and the women's meetings are held separately, joint sessions may be held at any time, by mutual consent.

These meetings, so instituted, are, no doubt, instrumental in bringing many more of the members into a larger sphere of usefulness, and into the exercise of their respective gifts in the church, the free course for which George Fox was so anxious to promote. With reference to this subject, he observes, in one of his epistles, "The least member in the church is serviceable, and all the members have need one of another."

While Friends are at liberty to exercise a prudent discretion, with respect to the admission of well disposed and serious persons, who are not members, to sit in our meetings for discipline, we advise that no persons under dealing for any misconduct, be allowed to sit in meetings for business, nor should their contribution be received, until they give satisfaction.

The Book of Discipline should be present in all our meetings for discipline, that it may be consulted or read, as occasion may require.

Meetings for business should endeavor to bring all subjects to a seasonable close; and when a meeting is unable to come to a satisfactory determination of any matter before it, it should apply to its superior meeting for its advice and assistance therein.

The minutes and reports, which go from inferior to superior meetings, should be signed by their clerks.

All the provisions in this article, or elsewhere in this book, in relation to the organization, management, and modes of proceeding of meetings for discipline, and all advices relative thereto, shall be construed as applying alike, to both men's and women's meetings, unless otherwise specifically provided.

THE YEARLY MEETING; ITS HISTORY, DESIGN, AND FUNCTIONS.

New England Yearly Meeting, being the first in America, was not set up like those of the present day, which have been set off from a parent stock, and organized at once, but gradually grew up as the Society grew; assuming more and more a definite form and organization, as the people, newly convinced, and as yet held together only by the bands of sympathy, love, and gospel unity, came to perceive their need. Rhode Island, in these times of persecution, was a place of quiet and Christian liberty; and Newport being easily accessible and constantly passed and repassed by the "*laborers*," in their journeys between New Amsterdam, Oyster Bay, and other localities southward, and Sandwich, Plymouth, Boston, Salem, and Piscataqua, at the eastward, became naturally the place of meeting, and this was favored still more, by the toleration, and even countenance of the authorities. The house of William Coddington, the Governor, soon became, and continued to be, the place of meetings, both for worship and discipline, until his death in 1688. As early as 1657, in the sixth month, five ministers from England landed at Newport from the little ship Woodhouse, and they, with the master, also a minister, were engaged in that vicinity from the 3d to the 12th of the month; but what meetings were held does not appear. In 1658, there were fifteen ministers laboring in New England, viz., eleven from England, three from Barbadoes, and one from Rhode Island. In the sixth month of this year, most of these were in prison in various places.

"In 1659," says Peter Pearson, "upon the 9th day of the 4th [now 6th] mo., and 4th day of the week, all of us, English Friends, that were abroad in the country, had a meeting upon Rhode Island."

1660. Persecution was sharp this year, and there is no account of any meeting. William Robinson, a merchant of London, and Marmaduke Stevenson, of Yorkshire, suffered death for truth's sake, on the 27th of 8th mo. In this year, Mary Dyer was hung. William Leddra was hung the 14th day of 1st mo., 1661.

"In 1661," says George Bishop, "a Yearly or general meeting was held on Rhode Island,* at which the people of Boston were much alarmed, fearing Friends were assembling to attack them." There is good reason to believe that the meeting was regularly held from this time. It was attended in 1671 by John Burnyeat, who says, "It begins the 9th of 4th [now 6th] mo. every year, and continues much of a week; and is a general meeting for Friends of New England." George Fox attended it in 1672, (the year the call was issued for the first Representative Yearly Meeting held in London,) and says it held six days; four for worship, one for the men's and one for the women's meeting for business, and that it was not a Yearly Meeting for New England only, but for other colonies adjacent; "including, doubtless," says Bowden, "Long Island, Jerseys, Maryland, and Virginia." In these, several men's and women's meetings for other parts were agreed upon and settled, to take care of the poor, and other affairs of the church, and to see that all who profess the truth, walk according to the glorious Gospel of God. *G. Fox's Journal, pp.* 156–7. But no records of the general meeting at this place are preserved, prior to 1683, when the following minutes appear, which are not only the oldest

---

* Where the meeting was then held does not appear, but in 1672 George Fox attended it, at the house of Gov. William Coddington, and probably from that time, certainly from 1683 to 1688, it was held at the same place; from 1689 to 1697 it was held at Walter Newbury's house; 1698 at his widow's, Anne Newbury's. In 1701, the record says, "Met at our meeting-house," and "On 6th day Public Friends had a meeting at 8 o'clock, at our old meeting-house, till 10 o'clock — then began our Yearly Meeting at our new meeting-house."

existing records of this meeting, but *all* the records of this session, viz.:

"It is Agreed on and settled at A general yearly meeting at the house of Wm. Coddington in Rhode Island, ye 11th 4th [6th] mo. 1683. — The yearly general meeting of Friends worshipping God, — Theare assembly at Rhoad Island Begins ye second daye of ye 4th [6th] month in every yeare, til friends see cause in ye wisdom and counsell of God to alter it.

"At Duxbury, ye generall yearley meeting Begins on ye last sixth daye in every 7th [9th] M: & since, it is altered to ye first 6th daye in every 8th [10th] month.

"At Piscatua ye generall meeting Begins ye second first-daye after duxbury meeting.

"At Salem ye generall meeting Begins ye next first-daye After duxbury meeting.

"At dartmo'h ye generall yearley meeting is to Begin ye 4th first daye After Duxbury meeting.

"At Warwick A yearley meeting is appoynted ye second first-day in every 3d [5th] mo."

These meetings are doubtless the same, or part of the same, referred to in the Journal of George Fox, as "settled" in 1672; but the times and places of holding them were now arranged in more definite order. The meeting at Sandwich,* one of the oldest and largest, is not named in the list, probably because the time was not changed. It was held on the third 6th day in the 1st [3d] mo. Nantucket meeting was not set up until 4th [6th] mo. 23d, 1708. Although the meeting at Newport, from the various causes alluded to, was more prominent, and gradually increased in relative importance, it does not appear to have differed in character from the general yearly meetings

---

* The meetings at Sandwich and Duxbury can be traced back to 1679.

held at Sandwich, Scituate, Salem, Piscataqua, &c., until 1693, when the following document was issued by it:

"At a general Yearly Meeting at the house of Walter Newbury on Rhode Island the 13th of 4th [6th] mo. 1693.

"The several particular meetings being called upon,

Rhode Island, \
Sandwich, \
Scituate, \
Salem, \
Piscataway, \
Oyster-Bay, } No business from any of them does present to this meeting.

"It is agreed at this meeting, that the weighty friends of the several meetings do appoint one or two faithful friends to attend this Yearly Meeting, and give their attendance at the usual place, on the 6th and 7th days, in the morning, by the 8th hour, before the public meeting of worship do begin; and bring in an account of sufferings, if any be, or other business that may relate to this meeting; and if the business is not ended then, the 2d day in the morning may be appointed, that all things may be done in order, and have reasonable time to end things that shall come before us."

The other "general meetings" within New England now began to be held quarterly, and soon took the name of Quarterly Meetings, agreeably to propositions made in 1686, 1687, and 1693, occupying an intermediate place and office, between the "Yearly Meeting for New England" and the monthly meetings. Two of the latter had been set up, viz., Sandwich, believed to be the oldest in America, as early as 1658, (when eighteen families recorded their names); and Duxbury, which is noticed in the Old Colony Records of 1660. Monthly meetings were not yet generally established in England, — but in

1666 and 1667 George Fox made special effort by "writing into all parts," as he says, "to stir up Friends to move in it, and establish their monthly meetings."

Following these "general meetings," in their change to quarterly meetings, we find, not a definite and decided change to the present organization, and subordination of inferior to superior meetings; nor to the present division of duties, or functions; but rather, a gradual growth or perfecting of the system through a series of years.

The name of "Duxbury General Yearly Meeting" was changed to Scituate, and then to Pembroke; but the meeting was soon after absorbed in Sandwich Quarterly Meeting, which, being held first as a yearly meeting, was, in 1685, held as a "Half Year's Meeting," but in 1686 was changed to a quarterly meeting, and dates from that time.

"Dartmouth General Meeting" was first included in Rhode Island Quarterly Meeting; and then set off to Sandwich in 1788.

"Warwick," or "Greenwich," and "Swanzy," were also soon included in Rhode Island Quarterly Meeting.

"Oyster Bay" was set off, and with other meetings was organized as New York Yearly Meeting, in 1695.

"Salem" took the name and form of Salem Quarterly Meeting, probably in 1687, at first including "Piscataqua," which was afterwards set off in 1815 as Dover Quarterly Meeting.

In all this work of organization, George Fox was not the only laborer, but rather a prominent instrument in "making ready a people prepared of the Lord." He was laboring in this country when the call for a representative Yearly Meeting was issued from London, by that Yearly Meeting of Ministers, in 1672. The fields were already white unto harvest, and George Fox, as a true servant of the Lord, sought not to be regarded as a leader, but pointed all to Christ as the Head; and exhorted all to pray to the Lord of the harvest, to send forth laborers into his harvest. And "many were raised up in various localities to preach the Gospel in its spirituality and fullness." As early as 1652, there were twenty-five ministers who gave themselves to the work in England, and multitudes were convinced. "In 1654, there were no less than sixty travelling in nearly all the counties of England and Wales, and in parts of Scotland and Ireland, and meetings for worship were established in most parts of the nation." And, notwithstanding the persecution, in a few years after, we find them earnestly engaged in all the colonies of this country, and some even among the aborigines.

THE DESIGN AND FUNCTIONS OF THE YEARLY MEETING.

It is called "The Yearly Meeting of Friends for New England," embracing in its limits all New England east of the Connecticut river.

The intent and design of our annual assemblies, in their first constitution, was, for the great and weighty oversight, and Christian care of the affairs of the churches, pertaining to our Christian communion, in all those things wherein we may be capable to serve one another in love.

In 1695, the records say, "The good and blessed intent and end of this and of all our assemblies, is, with the Lord's assistance, for his honor, in promoting and maintaining our Christian society and religion, in life and practice, in all the parts and branches thereof."

REGULATIONS.

The Yearly Meeting is to be held on Rhode Island, beginning with a meeting of Ministers and Elders at nine o'clock A. M., on the second sixth day of the sixth month, at Newport; the meeting for church discipline to begin at 9 o'clock on seventh day morning, at Newport; the meetings for worship on first day following, to begin at 10 o'clock in the morning, and at 4 o'clock in the afternoon, both at Portsmouth and Newport.

The clerks, or in their absence, the assistant clerks, shall act as clerks at the first session for discipline of the Yearly Meeting in each year. The representatives of the men's and women's meetings respectively shall meet at the close of such first session, and shall, when so met, nominate clerks and assistant clerks from among the members of the meeting. The said nominations shall be reported to the next session of the Yearly Meeting for confirmation, previously to any other business; and the clerks shall continue to serve until others are appointed.

No representative should withdraw from the meeting before it ends, without leave; that the service of the meeting may not be neglected.

All papers that come before the meeting, except such as are from its recognized official correspondents, shall be first examined by a committee appointed for the purpose, to determine the propriety of their introduction, before they are read in the meeting; and the same rule shall apply also to quarterly and monthly meetings.

Collections shall be made when called for by the meeting for defraying the expenses of the Society, and shall be lodged in the hands of a treasurer (to be annually appointed,) and shall be subject to be drawn out for its service by those properly authorized, who shall account for the same. The treasurer's accounts shall be audited annually by a committee of the Yearly Meeting appointed for that purpose.

The sums which may be thought necessary to be raised, shall be apportioned to each quarterly meeting by the representatives present; and each quarterly meeting is desired to be punctual in sending up the amount thereof accordingly.

The business of the Yearly Meeting should be conducted in the fear of God, without contention or striving; and with as few words, and in as pertinent expression to the matter in hand, as may be, for expediting the affairs thereof without loss of time, or in any way disturbing the meeting; one only at a time standing and speaking, that all things may be done decently and in order.

QUARTERLY MEETINGS.

A Quarterly Meeting shall consist of one or more monthly meetings, and shall extend a kind and tender Christian care over its subordinate meetings, and shall be subordinate to the Yearly Meeting. It shall be organized by the appointment annually of clerks, assistant clerks, and a treasurer, who shall serve until others are appointed to take their places.

Until further directed, the several quarterly meetings shall be held as follows, viz.: *Rhode Island quarter*, in the 8th month, at Newport, 11th month, at Fall River, 2d month, at Providence, and 5th month, at East Greenwich; on the first fifth-day in the month, at each place: *Salem quarter*, on the third fifth-day in the 1st month, at Salem; on the 4th fifth-day in the 5th month, at Amesbury; on the third fifth-day in the 8th month, at Lynn; on the 3d fifth-day in the 10th month, at Weare: *Sandwich quarter*, on the first fifth-day in the month; at New Bedford, in the 4th and 12th months, at Falmouth in the 7th, and at Sandwich in the 10th: *Falmouth quarter*, on the fifth-day before the first sixth-day in the month; at Windham, in the 2d and 9th, at Falmouth, Maine, in the 6th, and at Durham in the 11th month: *Smithfield quarter*, on the second fifth-day in the month; at Worcester in the 2d, at Northbridge in the 5th, at Bolton in the 8th, and at Smithfield in the 11th month: *Vassalborough quarter*, on the second sixth-day in the 2d, 9th and 11th months, and the last sixth-day in the 5th month; at Vassalborough, in the 2d and 9th months, and at East Vassalborough, in the 5th and 11th months: *Dover quarter*, on the fourth fifth-day in the month; at the upper meeting-house in Rochester, (Meaderborough,) in the 1st, at Dover in the 4th, at Sandwich, New Hampshire, in the 10th, and at North Berwick on sixth-day after the fourth fifth-day in the 8th month: *Fairfield quarter*, at Manchester, on fourth-day before the second sixth-day in the 2d and 9th months; at Fairfield on fourth-day before the last sixth-day in the 5th month, and at the same place on fourth-day before the second sixth-day in the 11th month. A meeting for divine worship shall be held on the first day of holding each quarterly meeting, preceding their opening the business, according to the ancient and general practice of Friends.

The several quarterly meetings shall transmit annually to the Yearly Meeting information of any meetings which have been settled, discontinued, or united in the course of the year; and when any quarterly meeting thinks it right, under special circumstances, to give permission to a monthly meeting to be held less frequently than once in the month, the same shall be reported to the Yearly Meeting. If any quarterly meeting shall, upon deliberate consideration, judge it right and expedient to lay down or dissolve any of the monthly meetings belonging thereto, and join the members thereof to another of its monthly meetings, it is authorized so to do; and the members of those dissolved meetings are to be accepted and recognized as under the care of the said meeting to which they are joined. And when a quarterly meeting hath come to a judgment on this or any other matter relative to any monthly meeting belonging to it, and notified the same in writing to such monthly meeting, the said monthly meeting ought to submit to the judgment of the quarterly meeting; but, if such monthly meeting shall not be satisfied therewith, then the monthly meeting may appeal to the Yearly Meeting, against the judgment and determination of the quarterly meeting.

And, if a monthly meeting shall refuse to take the advice and submit to the judgment of the quarterly meeting, and notwithstanding will not appeal against the determination of the said meeting to the Yearly Meeting; in such case, the quarterly meeting shall be at liberty either to dissolve such monthly meeting, or to bring the affair before the next or the succeeding Yearly Meeting. And, in case a quarterly meeting shall dissolve a monthly meeting, the dissolved monthly meeting, or any part thereof, in the name of the said meeting, shall be at liberty to appeal to the next or the succeeding Yearly Meeting, against such dissolution; but, if the dissolved monthly meeting, or a part thereof in its behalf, shall not appeal to the Yearly Meeting, the quarterly meeting shall join the members of the said late monthly meeting to such other monthly meeting as it may think most convenient; and, until such time, shall take care that no inconvenience doth thereby ensue to the members of such dissolved meeting, respecting any branch of our discipline. And, if any of the monthly meetings to which the quarterly meetings shall join the whole or a part of the late monthly meetings do think themselves aggrieved, they shall be at liberty to appeal against the quarterly meeting to the Yearly Meeting; and, until such appeal is heard and determined, the Friends added by the quarterly meeting to them shall be deemed their members.

All minutes and written epistles from the Yearly Meeting shall be entered by the quarterly meeting in books properly kept, that all Friends of the said quarter may have recourse to them, as occasion shall require.

Each quarterly meeting shall appoint two or more representatives to attend the Yearly Meeting.

The attention of quarterly meetings is recommended to the circumstances of the very small meetings for worship, and the small monthly meetings, within their limits. We desire that the condition of these meetings may obtain the care of well concerned Friends, and that a brotherly and christian intercourse, so far as is practicable, may be kept up between all the members of a quarterly meeting.

MONTHLY MEETINGS.

A Monthly Meeting consists of one or more preparative meetings, and holds its sittings monthly, and is subordinate to the quarterly meeting. Clerks and assistant clerks shall be appointed annually, to serve until others are chosen.

Each monthly meeting shall also appoint a treasurer, who shall keep a regular account of all moneys received and paid on behalf of the meeting. Also a correspondent, to authenticate all documents sent from one monthly or quarterly meeting to another.

Information of the appointment of correspondents shall be forwarded to the quarterly meeting, and by the quarterly meeting to the Yearly Meeting. A recorder shall also be annually appointed. (See article on Records.)

In every monthly meeting a proper number of faithful and judicious men and women Friends, belonging to each of the particular or preparative meetings, should be appointed to the station of overseers within the same; whose duty it is to exercise a vigilant and tender care over their fellow-members; that if anything repugnant to the harmony and good order of the Society appears among them, it may be timely attended to. And they are also entreated to be especially careful to maintain an upright life and unblamable conversation, that the advice which they give to others may be better received, and carry with it greater weight and force, on the minds of those whom they may be concerned to admonish.

In the selection of overseers the monthly meeting should appoint a joint committee of men and women Friends, to propose to the succeeding monthly meeting the names of one or more suitable men, and also of women Friends, in each preparative meeting, for that service; and the appointment of these overseers shall be by concurrent action of both meetings.

Notwithstanding overseers are appointed for a particular preparative meeting, yet, if circumstances require it, they may act in another preparative meeting belonging to the same monthly meeting.

The monthly meeting should also appoint two or more Friends, men and women, from each preparative meeting, as overseers of the poor, who shall attend to the necessities of those who may need assistance, and give such aid and advice as may appear needful.

Two or more Friends should be appointed annually, as auditors to settle the accounts of the treasurer, overseers of the poor, and of the trustees of all trust funds held by the meeting, or under its direction.

The foregoing appointments are to be made annually; but those appointed, and all others under annual appointment, shall serve until others are appointed in their stead.

Monthly meetings should appoint one or more Friends as representatives to each quarterly meeting, whose duty it is to attend to the seasonable dispatch and completion of the business intrusted to their care, taking with them what may be specially committed to them by the monthly meeting, which should be in writing.

The right to membership in the Society extends to any child born of parents in membership; to any child, of which either the father or mother is at the time of its birth a member, provided such father and mother were both of them members at the time of marriage; and to such as may have been admitted to the right, on request or otherwise.

Monthly meetings are at liberty, in their discretion, to admit into membership in their minority, any children whose parents are or may have been members, or who may be otherwise connected with our Society, in cases where a sincere desire is manifest to train and educate such children in accordance with our religious principles; and, when but one of the parents is a member of our Society, such are encouraged to bring up their children agreeably to Truth, as far as is in their power, and, when they think it suitable for them to be members, not to neglect asking the care of Friends in their behalf.

Although we recognize the children of our members as objects of our care, and partakers of the outward privileges of Christian fellowship, we would earnestly remind all, that such recognition cannot constitute them members of the church of Christ. Nothing can effect this but the power of the Holy Spirit working repentance towards God, and faith towards our Lord Jesus Christ: therefore, let the words of our Divine Master have their due place with us all: "Ye must be born again." May all our members become such, on the ground of true conversion and convincement, and be prepared in their several places to bring forth fruit unto God.

Requests from those who desire to be received into membership should be introduced through the preparative meeting, but the overseers may, in exceptional cases, to save time, bring such requests directly to the monthly meeting; and, in either case that meeting may appoint some suitable Friends, who shall inquire into the life and conversation of the applicants, and also take an opportunity for serious conference with them, the better to understand whether their motives for such request be sincere and from religious conviction, and make report of their suitableness to become members accordingly. If such report be satisfactory to the meeting, a record shall then be made of the acceptance of such persons as members of our society, and a committee be appointed to inform them thereof.

Monthly meetings are required to keep an alphabetical list of their members, and annually to appoint a committee for the purpose of examining such list, by comparing the entries on the monthly meeting's records, who shall also prepare an abstract of statistics, showing the number of births, deaths, removals into or out of the meeting, admissions by request, disowned, and the total number of members, in time to be forwarded through the quarterly meeting to the Yearly Meeting annually.

Monthly meetings are desired to maintain a correspondence with such of their members as have removed out of the reach of the oversight of their friends, and beyond the limits of any recognized meetings for discipline, so as to bring them under the Christian notice and sympathy of these meetings, and that they have a special regard to them, when their lists of members are annually read and revised; and absent members are desired to forward annually their address to the clerk of the monthly meeting to which they belong.

In case of resignation of membership, the monthly meeting, unless it should consider such action unnecessary, should appoint a committee to visit the person offering it, for the purpose of removing, if practicable, the cause of such resignation. If this labor prove unavailing, the meeting may release him from membership, and appoint a committee to inform him thereof, unless the circumstances of the case, in their judgment, require a testimony against him; but no objection shall be interposed, which is based on any alleged infraction of the discipline, heretofore committed, for which the meeting or its officers, having had reasonable opportunity so to do, has not taken him under dealing.

When any person requests to be admitted into membership with us, and when any member asks a dismissal, or is taken under dealing in a monthly meeting, the meeting, whether men's or women's, in which the business originates, shall acquaint the other meeting thereof, in order for their united sympathy and help, if they think it best; and when the meeting to which the application is made, or by which the member may be under dealing, is about to receive, restore, dismiss, or disown the person whose case is under consideration, both meetings should be acquainted therewith, and their concurrence be manifested, before the conclusion is entered; and when the approbation of both meetings is obtained, the same shall be entered on the minutes of both. And it is advised that men and women be attentive and ready in their meetings, to lend their assistance to each other, when it appears to be useful and best.

Monthly meetings should take special care, on suitable occasions, to appoint proper, prudent, and judicious Friends, to visit their brethren in their families, to inform, advise, or admonish, as circumstances may require, and such Friends should labor faithfully, in a spirit of love, and in the meekness of wisdom, to convince the judgments of the respective visited members of the necessity of their coming up with their brethren, in practice agreeably to our christian principles; that so, the several branches of the testimony given us to bear, may be maintained inviolate.

DELINQUENCIES. — Friends are earnestly exhorted in the love of Christ, to watch diligently over the flock, and labor seasonably, and in a spirit of Christian love and tenderness with all such as walk disorderly amongst us, in order to reclaim and restore them by brotherly counsel and admonition. When any one of our members shall have transgressed the rules of our discipline, and such due private labor has been bestowed without effect, information of the transgression should be communicated by the overseers, through the preparative meeting, to the monthly meeting. That meeting shall thereupon appoint some well qualified Friends to visit such member, and to inquire carefully into the matter, and labor for the restoration of the member thus transgressing. The Friends so appointed shall report in due time their care and labor in the case, when the monthly meeting may proceed to dispose of the same; and the person so labored with shall be informed of its decision, and, in case of disownment, of his right of appeal.

In case of the delinquency of a Friend who is not a member of the meeting in which he resides, care should be taken, after due inquiry and private labor, that the meeting to which he belongs be informed of the case. The meeting of which he is a member shall then proceed to visit and labor with him, unless by reason of distance it be not convenient; in which case it shall apply to the monthly meeting in which the delinquent resides to act for it, and visit him, and report its proceedings to the meeting of which he is a member; which meeting may then take such action thereon as in their judgment the case may seem to require, reporting its conclusion to the other meeting.

If said delinquent remove after the consideration of his case be commenced, the meeting that had him under its care shall continue the same, if he be equally within its reach; or otherwise, is at liberty to write to the meeting into the limits of which he is removed; which meeting may be requested to proceed therein, and report to the meeting of which he is a member; which meeting may then take such action thereon as in its judgment the case may require, as aforesaid.

If an individual commit an offence which the monthly meeting judge to be of such a nature as to require its speedy action for the clearing of truth, it is at liberty, on satisfactory evidence thereof, to proceed even to the disownment of the offender, without the appointment of a committee.

In case offenders shall remove to places not within the acknowledged limits of any monthly meeting, they may be placed under the care of the meeting to which they are nearest situated.

If an offender cannot be found after reasonable inquiry, the meeting to which he belongs shall issue a testimony against him, if the nature of the case require it.

In all proceedings for disorderly walking, the complaint shall be based on the discipline, as it stood when the alleged offence was committed; and no advice, rule, or regulation subsequently adopted, shall be allowed to influence the proceedings or decision thereon, to the disadvantage of the person offending.

If any member shall make, or countenance, any false entry of goods or merchandise, or in any other way attempt to defraud the public revenue, or intentionally buy or sell any goods, knowing them to have been falsely entered, or by incorrect returns or statements, or in any other way, seek to defraud the government, monthly meetings should labor with such as disorderly walkers.

When any of our members, either in courts or elsewhere, violate our testimony by either taking or administering oaths, monthly meetings are desired to extend brotherly labor towards them, and, if they cannot be prevailed upon to give satisfaction, to testify their disunity with them.

Friends cannot consistently with our well known principles against all wars and fighting, engage in any preparation or combination of a warlike or military character whatever, nor in any occupation or business pursuit, the object of which is to contribute to the support of war, nor can they procure substitutes, nor pay any war tax or contribution, in lieu of personal service. Should any of our members depart from a consistent maintenance of our testimonies in these respects, tender advice should be extended to them, in order for their convincement and restoration, and, should this labor prove ineffectual, monthly meetings should proceed to disown them.

As it is not consistent with our testimony against war, for any of our members to receive pensions for military services from the government, though they may be reduced to necessitous circumstances, this necessity should be relieved by monthly meetings, who will thereby preserve our religious testimony against the anti-christian practice of war, and manifest their sympathy for their brethren by contributing to their comfortable support.

A tender care should be exercised by Friends over one another for good, and should they observe any to be deficient in discharging their just debts in due time, or neglecting to keep their word, promises, or engagements, in their dealings, or should any trade beyond their ability, and thus give reasonable suspicion of inability or negligence; such should be seasonably advised or cautioned herein, in order for their help or improvement; and if any proceed contrary to such advice, or by their failure bring reproach upon the church, Friends may justifiably proceed to testify against such offenders.

If any of our members absent themselves from our religious meetings, and disregard the repeated advice and endeavors of Friends to induce them to attend to this important duty, they should be tenderly treated with for their restoration, by the monthly meeting to which they belong.

It being recommended to the representative meeting to take the oversight of all writings proposed to be printed, relating to our religious principles or testimonies, for which the society is to be held responsible, our members who may have any such publications in view, are required to lay them before said meeting for its advice and concurrence. And if any of our members shall print or publish any such writing against the advice of said meeting, such persons shall be complained of to the monthly meeting to which they belong, and if they cannot be convinced of the impropriety of their conduct, and led to condemn the same, to the satisfaction of said meeting, they should be disowned, as opposed to the peace and good order of the society.

Friends are cautioned against printing, publishing, or circulating any writings which may be hurtful in their tendency, or which may excite disunity or discord, and where any disregard this advice monthly meetings should deal with them as offenders.

If a member of our society shall accept any office in the civil government, such as is advised against in the article on that subject, and shall persevere in conduct thus adverse to our principles, such case should be reported for action to the monthly meeting.

If any member of our society shall arrest, sue, or implead at law, any other member thereof, except in cases provided in the article on Differences and Arbitrations, and except also in the case provided below, such person should be dealt with for the same, by the meeting to which he belongs; and if he shall not give satisfaction for such disorderly proceedings, he may be disowned by the meeting. Or, if the party so sued or arrested, taking with him, or, if under confinement, sending, one or two Friends to the person who goes to law, shall complain thereof, the said person shall be required immediately to stay proceedings; and, if he do not comply with such requisition, the monthly meeting to which he belongs may disown him if the case require it. But, in case there is good reason to believe that a debtor is about to remove himself, or his effects, for the purpose of defrauding his creditors, or to avoid the payment of his just dues, or by any other means is attempting to effect such purpose, the prohibition of resort to legal process shall not apply; and, in such case, the monthly meeting is the proper judge of the circumstances, and should see that justice is done between the parties concerned.

With regard to the attendance at stage plays, horse races, entertainments of music and dancing, or being engaged in lotteries, wagering, or other species of gaming; when any of our members are found engaging therein, or are in the practice of any immorality, or other reproachful conduct, the monthly meeting where such transgressors belong should deal with them.

Our members are affectionately and earnestly advised not to connect themselves with any secret societies, even though they may profess to be instituted for the promotion of good and benevolent objects. And when the cause of truth appears likely to suffer from a disregard of this advice, the case should be reported to the monthly meeting for action thereon.

MINISTERS. — The following order is to be observed in acknowledging the gift of any Friend in the ministry.

Where any Friend appears in public ministry whose life and conversation shall be clean and blameless, and the monthly meeting, within the limits of which the Friend belongs, is convinced that the Lord hath called him or her to that weighty work, the name having been introduced by a committee appointed by the monthly meeting for that purpose, or by the preparative meeting of ministers and elders, through its clerk, and the monthly meeting being united in approving him or her as a minister in the church, it shall acquaint the quarterly meeting therewith, which, after solidly waiting for the concurring unity of men and women Friends, and finding nothing to hinder, shall minute the same, and acquaint the quarterly meeting of ministers and elders thereof, which shall also enter the acknowledgment on its minutes, as, from the period of their acknowledgment, they become members of that meeting. Information of such acknowledgment shall be given by the quarterly meeting to the person so acknowledged, and to the Yearly Meeting, and by the Yearly Meeting, through its clerk, to the Yearly Meeting of ministers and elders, and the names are to be entered on the records of those meetings.

Should the monthly meeting desire assistance in this proceeding, after having appointed a judicious committee of men and women Friends, application may be made to the quarterly meeting, which shall appoint a few Friends, both men and women, who, with those appointed by the monthly meeting, shall form a committee for judging of the gifts and qualifications of such as may be thus proposed for this important station. Their report shall be presented to the monthly meeting for its consideration and decision, the same as in the former case.

If any Friend appearing as a minister shall give cause of uneasiness or dissatisfaction in doctrine, behavior, conversation or ministry, the person so offending should be treated with privately, in a gospel spirit and manner. If this shall not take effect, let complaint be made of such person to the monthly meeting to which he or she may belong, in order that proceedings thereon may be had accordingly, and the matter be settled with all suitable expedition.

Monthly meetings should be careful that all Friends travelling from or among them in the work of the ministry, go in the unity of the meeting to which they belong, and with written testimonials therefrom; and monthly meetings are advised to take due care in giving such testimonials, in order to prevent the uneasiness which sometimes falls on the church from an unqualified ministry.

None should travel abroad as ministers, without having been first recommended to the quarterly meeting, and accepted by it as such, and none should appoint meetings out of the limits of the quarterly meeting they belong to, without a certificate from the monthly meeting or the concurrence thereof.

When any ministers have a concern to travel in the work of the ministry, and to appoint meetings out of the quarterly meeting they belong to, or to attend the sittings of other yearly meetings, or of meetings belonging thereunto, they should seasonably communicate information of the same to the preparative meeting of ministers and elders to which they belong, (for which purpose a special meeting may be called, if necessary,) for its consent to lay the concern before the monthly meeting. If such consent is obtained, they should then apply to their monthly meeting for a written testimonial of its concurrence, which, if it be granted, shall be prepared and signed by the clerks and correspondent of the monthly meeting; and monthly meetings are requested to take care that Friends, to whom certificates or minutes to travel have been issued, return them seasonably. When such concern extends to visiting the churches within any other yearly meeting on this continent, they should proceed in like manner. And, when the monthly meeting has given its certificate, they should acquaint the quarterly meeting therewith, for its concurrence, which must be had before the Friend proceeds. When the concern is for a general or extensive visit, or to a foreign land, or beyond sea, it is recommended that the approbation of the Yearly Meeting of ministers and elders should likewise be obtained, unless such considerations as the monthly and quarterly meetings may judge sufficient shall prevent.

ELDERS. — Monthly meetings are desired to look carefully, from time to time, among their own members, and endeavor, under the influence of the Holy Spirit, to seek for such, not ministers, as give evidence that the gifts and qualifications necessary to fit them for the station of elders in the church have been conferred upon them, in order for their recognition and appointment to that weighty and important service. In this engagement neither age nor wealth should influence the choice, but such should be appointed as fear God, love his truth in sincerity, are sound in Christian doctrine, and are of clean hands.

In the appointment of elders, the following order should be observed. Let the monthly meeting, after it has approved such as it adjudges duly anointed and qualified for that service, (the name or names having been introduced by a joint committee, appointed by the monthly meeting for that purpose, or by the preparative meeting of ministers and elders, through its clerk,) acquaint the quarterly meeting thereof; and further proceedings in the case shall be the same as are provided in the case of ministers. Friends are advised, in these proceedings, to be weighty in their spirit and careful in their conversation, that no harm may come to the individual or to the church, from a disclosure before the time, of what may be under consideration, that all may be kept in the love and unity of the gospel.

If monthly meetings desire assistance in this concern, they should apply to the quarterly meeting, as directed in the case of ministers.

Monthly meetings are at liberty, after the exercise of due care and admonition, to displace such elders as appear to be either disqualified or unfaithful.

MEMORIALS.

Monthly meetings are advised to appoint suitable Friends to prepare memorials or minutes concerning deceased Friends, whether ministers or others, whose lives have been marked by devotedness to the cause of their Lord, and to the service of the church. In drawing up such documents, monthly meetings are desired to pay due regard to conciseness, and especially to bear in mind that the object is not eulogy, but to preserve a record of the power of divine grace in the lives of the Lord's faithful servants. Such testimonies, when drawn up, are to be presented by the monthly meeting to its quarterly meeting, which meeting is recommended in each case to revise the testimony so presented, (by a committee appointed for the purpose, or otherwise,) and it is left to the discretion of the quarterly meeting, either to send forward the same or a new testimony, prepared by itself, to the representative meeting, or if thought expedient, to withhold altogether any such testimony. Testimonies thus prepared, when approved by the representative meeting, shall be laid before the Yearly Meeting to be read and recorded.

PREPARATIVE MEETINGS.

Each established meeting for worship shall be a preparative meeting, except in cases when the monthly meeting deems it expedient to unite two or more meetings for worship in one preparative meeting.

The preparative meeting shall hold a sitting preceding the monthly meeting to which it belongs, and shall be subordinate to the monthly meeting.

It shall read and consider the queries and advices, as settled by the Yearly Meeting, and conclude on written answers to the queries, essays of which should be submitted by the overseers, and these answers, when adopted, should be sent to the monthly meeting.

Applications from persons desiring to become members of our religious society should be made in writing to the monthly meeting, through the preparative meeting; or, when circumstances render such course inconvenient, such applications may be made directly to the monthly meeting, through the overseers.

Neither the preparative meeting, nor the overseers, may judge of a request for membership so as to prevent its going to the monthly meeting, though either may call the attention of the applicant to any manifest obstruction: but should he continue desirous to have it laid before the monthly meeting, it should be forwarded accordingly.

Information of any difference between members which the overseers are unable to reconcile, or complaints against any member, must also be submitted to the preparative meeting in writing, signed by two or more of the overseers; and such business as may require the care of the monthly meeting should be forwarded to that meeting without unnecessary delay.

All complaints made by the overseers should be submitted by them to the preparative meeting, which body, if it approve thereof, should forward the same to the monthly meeting; and when the overseers believe it right to carry a complaint, or information respecting the conduct of any member, to the preparative meeting, timely notice should be given to the party, when it can reasonably be done, previously to its being laid before the preparative meeting.

It is advised that, in general, two representatives be appointed by each preparative meeting, to attend the monthly meeting.

Small preparative meetings, at the discretion of the monthly meeting, may be permitted to act as a united preparative meeting of men and women Friends. The answers to the queries therefrom should be sent, both to the men's and women's monthly meeting, and representatives appointed to each, when practicable.

When the monthly meeting consists of but one particular meeting, the preparative meeting may be dispensed with, if deemed expedient by the monthly meeting.

It is apprehended that advantage might be derived from occasionally reading, in preparative meetings, portions of the counsel contained in the book of discipline.

GENERAL ADVICES.

These are to be read in the monthly meetings, either consecutively, or in such portions, as well as at such times, as may be deemed by them most desirable.

Take heed, dear Friends, we entreat you, to the convictions of the Holy Spirit, who leads, through unfeigned repentance and living faith in the Son of God, to reconciliation with our Heavenly Father, and to the blessed hope of eternal life, purchased for us by the one offering of our Lord and Saviour Jesus Christ.

Be earnestly concerned, in your religious meetings, reverently to present yourselves before the Lord, and to seek, by the help of the Holy Spirit, to worship God in spirit and in truth.

Prize the privilege of access by Him unto the Father; continue "instant in prayer," and "watch in the same with thanksgiving."

Be in the frequent practice of waiting upon the Lord in private retirement, honestly examining yourselves as to your growth in grace, and your preparation for the life to come.

Be diligent in the private perusal of the Holy Scriptures; and let it be your earnest endeavor that the daily reading of them in your families be devoutly conducted.

Be careful to make a profitable and religious use of those portions of time, on the first day of the week, which are not occupied by our meetings for worship.

Live in love as Christian brethren, ready to be helpful one to another, sympathizing with each other in the trials and afflictions of life, and manifesting an earnest desire that each may possess a well grounded hope in Christ.

Watch over one another for good. When occasions of uneasiness first appear in any, let them be treated with, in privacy and tenderness, before the matter is communicated to another. Should differences arise, be willing early to avail yourselves of the advice and judgment of your brethren; and may Friends be ready to undertake, and be prudent in executing, the blessed office of peacemaker.

Cherish a Christian interest on behalf of such attenders of your meetings as are not in membership; evincing a lively concern for their religious welfare, and growth in the truth.

Follow peace with all men, desiring the true happiness of all; be kind and liberal to the poor, and endeavor to promote the temporal, moral, and religious well-being of your fellow-men.

With a tender conscience, and in accordance with the precepts of the gospel, take heed to the limitations of the Spirit of Truth, in the pursuit of the things of this life.

Maintain strict integrity in your transactions in trade, and in all your outward concerns. Guard against a spirit of speculation, and the snare of accumulating wealth. Remember that you will have to account for the mode of acquiring, as well as for the manner of using, your possessions; and be equitable and judicious in the final disposition of them.

In contemplating the engagement of marriage, look principally to that which will help you on your heavenward journey. Pay filial regard to the judgment of your parents. Bear in mind the vast importance, in such a union, of an accordance in religious principles and practice. Ask counsel of God; desiring, above all temporal considerations, that your union may be owned and blessed of the Lord.

Watch, with Christian tenderness, over the opening minds of your children; inure them to habits of self-restraint and filial obedience; carefully instruct them in the knowledge of the Holy Scriptures; and seek for ability to imbue their hearts with the love of their Heavenly Father, their Redeemer, and their Sanctifier.

Be careful to maintain in your conduct, and to encourage in your families, that simplicity in deportment and attire, that avoidance of flattery and insincerity of language, and that nonconformity to the world, which become the disciples of the Lord Jesus.

Guard watchfully against the introduction into your households of publications of a hurtful tendency. Observe simplicity and moderation in the furniture of your houses, and in your style and manner of living.

Avoid such vain sports and places of diversion as are hurtful in their tendency, all kinds of gambling, the unnecessary frequenting of taverns and other public houses, and the use of intoxicating liquors; and guard against such companionships, indulgences, and recreations, as by their influence may interfere with your growth in grace.

Finally, dear Friends, let your conversation be as it becometh the gospel. Exercise yourselves to have always a conscience void of offence toward God and toward men; endeavoring to maintain the unity of the Spirit, in the bond of peace.

QUERIES.

Our members are reminded that the intention of directing queries to be answered, relative to the conduct of individuals, in the several branches of our Christian profession, is not only for the purpose of being informed of the state of our meetings, but also to impress on the minds of Friends a profitable examination of themselves, to determine how far they act consistently with their religious principles. 'Every member therefore is earnestly recommended, more especially when the answers are under consideration, to examine whether he, himself, is coming up in that life of self-denial and devotedness unto God, which so highly becomes all who make profession of the name of Christ. Yet, it is not to arrangements however perfect, but to individual faithfulness to Christ, in daily dependence upon the help of the Holy Spirit, that we must look for growth in the truth, and vitality in the church. As this faithfulness and dependence are maintained, we believe these queries will tend to promote the religious welfare of our members, and to the upholding of our Christian discipline in a lively and healthy condition.

NOTE.—This paragraph is to be read in those preparative and monthly meetings, in which *all* the queries are directed to be read and answered, previously to entering upon them.

QUERY 1. Are all meetings for religious worship and discipline regularly held? Do Friends attend them duly, and at the hour appointed; and are they preserved from unbecoming behavior therein?

QUERY 2. Are love and unity maintained among you? Is detraction guarded against? And, when any differences arise, are endeavors used to end them speedily?

QUERY 3. Are Friends careful to maintain a religious life and conversation? And, do those who have children or others under their care, endeavor, by example and precept, to train them up in accordance with our Christian profession?

QUERY 4. Do Friends frequently read the Holy Scriptures, individually, as well as collectively in their families, encouraging their children and others in the daily practice of this religious duty? Do they faithfully maintain our testimony to a free gospel ministry?

QUERY 5. Do Friends abstain from the use of intoxicating liquors as a beverage? Are they careful to avoid amusements and diversions inconsistent with a Christian character; and to observe true moderation in all things?

QUERY 6. Are the circumstances of the poor, and of such as appear likely to need assistance, duly inspected, and their necessities relieved? Are they assisted in obtaining suitable employment? And is proper care taken to educate their children?

QUERY 7. Do Friends faithfully maintain our testimony against bearing arms and other military matters; against oaths, and against defrauding the public revenue?

QUERY 8. Do Friends frequently inspect their affairs and settle their accounts? Are they punctual to their promises, and just in the payment of their debts, and careful to live within the bounds of their circumstances?

QUERY 9. Are Friends careful to have all their marriages, births, deaths, and burials duly recorded? Are there any Friends removed from, or come amongst you, without certificates?

Query 10. Is the discipline administered in christian tenderness, timely and impartially? And is judgment placed, when it appears necessary, in the authority of Truth, and according to discipline?

The answers to the queries should be full and explicit, comprising the substance of every part of each query, in order that the superior meeting, being rightly informed of the state of the church in general, may duly administer the needful advice and assistance.

It is also directed, that, to this purpose, the queries be first read in the preparative meetings preceding the quarterly meeting, and distinct answers be given in said meetings, to the first, second, and tenth; except previous to the spring quarter, when all are to be answered; and these answers are to be carried to their respective monthly meetings, where the queries are also to be read, and the answers aforesaid; and those answers digested in each monthly meeting, and sent thence to the quarterly meeting, where the queries are to be again read, and the answers thereto, which came from the monthly meetings; and a summary account made in the spring quarterly meeting, comprehending the state thereof, founded on the answers to all the queries, should be entered on their records, and transmitted to the yearly meeting, and there read. A summary of these reports should be entered in the yearly meeting record.

UNANSWERED QUERIES.

In order to realize the benefit of serious self-examination, and to induce an earnest desire to promote the good of others, the four following queries shall be read in preparative and monthly meetings at least once in the year, at such time as by these meetings may be deemed the most desirable; and are to be then seriously and deliberately considered, but not answered.

1. What is the religious state of your meeting; and is there among you evidence of a growth in the truth?

2. Are you individually giving evidence of true conversion of heart; of love to Christ, and self-denying devotedness to Him; and of a growing preparation for the life to come?

3. Do you maintain a watchful care against conformity to the world; against the love of ease and self-indulgence, or being unduly absorbed by your outward concerns to the hindrance of your religious progress; bearing in mind that "here have we no continuing city?"

4. Do you in gospel love seek to arouse the careless and indifferent, and to bring back those that go astray? Do you exercise a religious care over your younger members, manifesting an earnest concern that, through the power of Divine grace, they may all become established in the faith and hope of the gospel?

OVERSIGHT.

Very early after the rise of this Religious Society, which had been drawn from a dependence upon outward ceremonials to the immediate teachings of the Holy Spirit in the heart, care was manifested therein, in accordance with the practice of the primitive christians, that all its members might be preserved in unity together, and in a diligent occupation of the gifts conferred upon each. Gathered together by a Divine Hand, and taught to love as brethren, they were also engaged to watch over each other for good. The writings of George Fox contain frequent allusions to the concern which he felt, that all those who had been enlightened by the day-spring from on high, which had visited their souls, should not only walk worthy of the vocation wherewith they had been called, but should labor, under right qualification, for the help and encouragement of the different members of the body. "As the church of God in those days increased," said Stephen Crisp, "my care daily increased, and the weight of things relating both to the outward and inward condition of poor Friends, came upon me; the more I came to feel and perceive the love of God and his goodness to me, the more was I humbled and bowed in my mind to serve Him, and to serve the least of his people among whom I walked; and, as the word of wisdom began to spring in me, and the word of God grew, so I became a counsellor of those who had been tempted in like manner as I had been."

When one christian, in this spirit, reproves another for his fault, and thus endeavors to restore him to the fold of Christ, this is no improper interference with individual liberty, — it is but one legitimate fruit of the law of love; and not only is the duty incumbent "to warn them that are unruly," but also to "comfort the feeble minded," to "support the weak," and "be patient toward all men."

"Now concerning gospel order," said George Fox, "though the doctrine of Jesus Christ requireth his people to admonish a brother or sister twice before they tell the church, yet that limiteth none, so that they shall use no longer forbearance. Let such as behold their brother or sister in a transgression, go not in a rough, light, or upbraiding spirit, to reprove such, but in the power of the Lord and spirit of the Lamb, and in the wisdom and love of the Truth, which suffers thereby, to admonish such an offender. So may the soul of such a brother or sister be seasonably and effectually reached and overcome, and have cause to bless the name of the Lord on their behalf, and so a blessing may be rewarded into the bosom of that faithful and tender brother or sister, who so admonished them."

As you are concerned for the maintenance of good order in the church, keep your own hands clean and garments unspotted, that you may rebuke, if need be, with authority; and, being clothed with meekness and gentleness, steadily persevere in the discharge of the duty committed to you. Thus, the ignorant may be informed, the weak strengthened, the tender encouraged, the scattered sought out, and the unwary cautioned. May you exercise a tender care over our younger members, bearing in mind the exposed situation of many of these at this critical period of life. Cultivate an acquaintance with them; call upon them at their places of abode; and manifest, by the general tenor of your conduct towards them, a kind interest in their welfare, and a solicitude that they may be established upon the right foundation, — the faith and hope of the gospel. Encourage them to a diligent perusal of the Holy Scriptures, with desires that these may be blessed to their spiritual instruction.

This care and interest, one for another, is highly conducive to the welfare and growth of the church. Those who may be called to the ministry of the word should be diligent in their gifts, and faithful to their calling; instant in season, out of season, exhorting with all long-suffering and doctrine. Let the elders consider the importance of their position, that upon them, in great measure, rests the burden of the church, and that, although no unimportant part of their duty is to encourage ministers, and particularly to help forward those who are young in the work, yet their various services to the whole body are scarcely less than are included in the comprehensive charge of the Apostle to the assembled officers of the Ephesian church: "Take heed to yourselves, and to all the flock, over the which the Holy Ghost hath made you overseers, to feed the church of God, which he hath purchased with his own blood." And, may you that are in the station of overseers remember that, while your various duties may not be distinctly defined, yet the right performance of these duties is essential to the church, and may be a means of your own advancement in the spiritual life. May the sick and afflicted claim your assiduous care, and may those who are struggling with the perplexities or pecuniary losses incident to trade and business receive your sympathy and friendly advice. Should you have reason to fear that any of this class are going behind hand in their business concerns, be prompt to render, in christian freedom, and without intrusion, such counsel or help as may tend to raise them out of their present difficulty; or otherwise, to place them in such open relation to their creditors as shall lead to an amicable settlement of their affairs, and thus avert much of the suffering, and even the scandal, often attendant upon the unaided efforts of these to relieve themselves from pecuniary embarrassment. May you be careful to encourage in all, and especially in the young, the diligent attendance of our religious meetings; and particularly, may you endeavor to guard faithfully against a breach of that fellowship and unity between the different members of the body, so becoming the christian, and so essential to a religious growth. And may all, whatever may be your station in the church, strive to be fellow-helpers one of another, seeking to provoke unto love and to good works, and "as every man hath received the gift, even so minister the same one to another, as good stewards of the manifold grace of God."

MINISTERS AND ELDERS.

We are fully persuaded that the ministry of the gospel is not received of man, but by the revelation of Jesus Christ, according to that apostolical direction, "As every man hath received the gift, even so minister the same one to another;" "if any man speak let him speak as the oracles of God; if any man minister, let him do it as of the ability which God giveth, that God in all things may be glorified." And as this ministry is of divine origin, the motives and inducements thereunto should be disinterested, and no way mercenary, but concurrent with the precept Christ gave to his apostles and immediate followers: "Freely ye have received, freely give."

As to the elders among you, and those whom God, having indued with knowledge and experience of the cleansing operation of his spirit, hath concerned to minister unto others, let them adorn the doctrine of the gospel, by showing, out of a good conversation, their works, with meekness of wisdom. Such as these, being clothed with humility, and being exemplary to the flock whom they feed not by constraint, but willingly —" not for filthy lucre, but of a ready mind —" are worthy of double honor, and to be highly esteemed in the church of Christ.

If any one who has been a public minister, or elder, shall be guilty of such practices as may justly deserve public censure, and shall be disowned, and afterwards, upon tokens of repentance, be again admitted into membership, such readmission shall not be interpreted so as to give him or her the liberty of appearing as a public minister, or of exercising the office of an elder, until the monthly meeting they belong to shall judge the scandal, given by such person, to be so far removed, that such public ministry, or exercising the office of an elder, may not administer occasion of reproach, either from Friends or others. And should any show themselves forward in so appearing, the meeting to which they belong is desired to give them such advice as it shall deem suitable to the circumstances.

Where it shall appear, upon due inspection made, that any minister or elder neglects, or omits, the due attendance of meetings for worship or discipline, through sloth, indolence, love of the world, lukewarmness in religion, or other cause, the monthly meeting should take care that all such be timely visited in love, and acquainted with the desire of Friends in that case, and admonished to faithfulness therein. And if, notwithstanding the due christian labor and admonition, he shall continue in the said neglect or omission, if a minister, his public testimony should be denied; and if an elder, he should be dismissed from that station.

MEETINGS OF MINISTERS AND ELDERS.

As much depends on the conduct and example of ministers and elders, meetings have been established amongst them for the purpose of examining whether they all maintain an exemplary life, answerable to their station. The meetings of ministers and elders are constituted and held in the following manner: a clerk for each is to be appointed annually, and records of the proceedings should be carefully preserved.

Preparative Meetings. — The ministers and elders of each monthly meeting compose a preparative meeting of ministers and elders, (unless the quarterly meeting for discipline, from some peculiar circumstances, should judge it most advisable that it be constituted of the ministers and elders of more than one monthly meeting,) and meet once in three months, at some time previous to the monthly meeting, which immediately precedes the quarterly meeting; in which meetings, after some time spent in solid retirement, the queries addressed to ministers and elders are to be read, considered, and then and there answered in writing, and such answers forwarded to the quarterly meeting of ministers and elders. Opportunity may here also be given for tender advice and assistance, as the nature of any case may require; and representatives, taken from the members in either station, should be appointed to attend the quarterly meeting of ministers and elders.

Quarterly Meetings. — A quarterly meeting of ministers and elders, composed of the representatives from the preparative meetings, and of the other approved ministers and elders of the quarterly meeting, shall be held on the day preceding each quarterly meeting for discipline, at which meeting the queries are to be read, and the answers thereto from its subordinate meetings; to which latter meetings such advice should be extended as circumstances may require. A list of the names of all the ministers and elders of the several monthly meetings shall be kept by this meeting, and annually revised.

At the quarterly meeting of ministers and elders next preceding the Yearly Meeting, general answers are to be drawn up, to be sent by at least two representatives to the yearly meeting of ministers and elders, which yearly meeting is also to be furnished with the names of these representatives, together with a report in writing of the regular holding of the quarterly meeting of ministers and elders during the year.

Yearly Meeting. — A Yearly meeting of ministers and elders shall be held at Newport, on the day preceding the first sitting of the Yearly Meeting, at 9 o'clock in the morning, which meeting shall consist of the representatives from the quarterly meetings of ministers and elders, and such recorded ministers and appointed elders of the Yearly Meeting as may be in Newport at the time. This meeting may be continued from time to time, by adjournments, provided such adjournments do not interfere with the sittings of the Yearly Meeting, and that such meeting do not in any wise take upon it, or interfere with, any part of the discipline of the church, belonging either to the Yearly Meeting, or to any subordinate meeting. The meeting shall receive and read the answers to the queries from the quarterly meetings of ministers and elders, by which an opportunity will be given to impart such advice as shall be necessary; and, after having informed itself, by means of the answers received, of the state of the ministers and elders in the several quarterly meetings, it shall lay annually before the Yearly Meeting a summary, yet clear, account thereof.

QUERIES OF THE YEARLY MEETING OF MINISTERS AND ELDERS.

The three introductory Queries are to be read and weightily considered, but not answered.

The other four are to be answered in writing to the quarterly meeting of ministers and elders, and, in the spring, to the yearly meeting of ministers and elders.

Are ministers and elders engaged to watch unto prayer, that they may themselves be preserved in humble dependence upon Christ, and in an earnest religious exercise for the conversion of sinners, and for the edifying of the body in the faith and love of the gospel?

Are ministers and elders concerned faithfully to occupy the spiritual gifts entrusted to them, to the honor of God?

Are ministers, in the exercise of their gifts, careful to wait for Divine ability, and are they preserved thereby from being burdensome?

1. Are ministers and elders diligent in attending their meetings for worship and discipline, and careful to promote the attendance of their families?

2. Are the lives and conversation of ministers and elders clean and blameless amongst men? Are they in unity one with another, and with the meeting to which they belong, harmoniously laboring together for the honor of truth?

3. Are they careful to rule their own houses well; and do they endeavor, by example and precept, to train up their families in a religious life and conversation, consistent with our Christian profession?

4. Are they preserved in love; administering encouragement or counsel, as occasion may require, in reference to ministry or conduct?

☞ *The following advice should be read after the reading and consideration of the queries and answers:*

It is earnestly and affectionately recommended, that ministers and elders watch over one another for good, that they help those that are young in the ministry, discouraging forward spirits, that run into words without life and power, advising against affectation of tones and gestures, and every thing that would hurt their service; yet encouraging the humble, careful traveler, speaking a word in season to them that are weary. And let all dwell in that which gives ability to labor successfully in the church of

Christ, adorning the doctrine they deliver to others, being examples to the believers, in word, in conversation, in charity, in spirit, in faith and in purity.

REPRESENTATIVE MEETING.

The Yearly Meeting, in view of the necessity of having a representation during the time intervening between its yearly sessions, appoints annually a committee, to act as a representative meeting, which shall consist of not less than twenty-five members. It is entrusted with a general care of whatever may arise during the intervals of the Yearly Meeting, affecting our religious society, and requiring immediate attention.

The appointment of the representative meeting shall be made by the Yearly Meeting, on nomination thereto, by the representatives of the men's and women's meetings, the confirmation thereof to be by the concurrent action of both bodies; and, when any portion of the nomination, so made, is not confirmed, the subject shall be recommitted to the representatives, to give an opportunity for the substitution of other names in the place of those omitted.

Considering the nature and importance of the affairs which may claim the attention of the representative meeting, it is necessary that it be composed of such as are of clear discernment and clean hands, who adorn the doctrine they profess, in their lives and conversation.

Members of this meeting are desired to attend its sessions diligently, or, as often as circumstances will admit; and, if any member is prevented from attending any session, he should forward to the same his excuse therefor.

The duties of the representative meeting are, to correspond with similar committees of other Yearly Meetings; to examine testimonies concerning Friends deceased, and similar papers issued by our subordinate meetings; also manuscripts of a doctrinal character submitted by individual members or others; and, in general, to represent the Yearly Meeting in all cases where the reputation and interest of our religious society are concerned: but, in the exercise of these functions, it shall not meddle with matters of faith and discipline, not already determined by the Yearly Meeting. It shall, also take cognizance of all grievances arising amongst us, wherein any Friend may be affected in person or property, in regard to our christian testimony, to advise, counsel, and assist, as best wisdom may direct; and any aggrieved Friend or Friends may apply to it for that purpose.

This meeting should take care to provide suitable books for distribution, in such manner and in such places as it may judge proper, and particularly in the families of the poor, and such among us as are destitute of this means of instruction.

The meeting is authorized to draw upon the treasurer of the Yearly Meeting, in its recess, for such sums of money as occasion may from time to time require, being accountable for the same, and keeping records of all its proceedings; which records shall annually be laid before the Yearly Meeting, or such committee as it may appoint to inspect the same.

Regular meetings of the representative meeting shall be held at such times as may be determined upon at the first session after its annual appointment; and special meetings may be held on any emergency, at the written request of any five of the members thereof, reasonable notice being given to the members, as fully as is practicable, especially in matters of importance. At least ten members are necessary to constitute a meeting for action.

Should less than fifteen be present, it is required that they should be unanimous on all measures determined.

CARE OF THE POOR.

We have ever deemed it a commendable and christian practice, of good report, to care for and assist our own poor, to relieve their wants, and to comfort the afflicted among us, thereby improving the opportunity of doing good, especially to the household of faith. In watching over one another for good, as christian brethren and as Friends, seeking to be helpers one of another, in our moral and spiritual welfare, there should also be a kind and watchful care over those who need assistance, or may appear likely to need it, in their outward affairs, that their necessities may be relieved, either by counsel or pecuniary aid, as the case may require, and they be assisted in such business as they are capable of; and, that their children may so partake of learning, as to fit them for the active duties of life. It ought to be considered, that the poor, both parents and children, are of our family, and ought not to be turned off to any others, for their support or education; and the rich should remember, it is more blessed to give than to receive, and that "he who hath pity on the poor, lendeth to the Lord, and that which he hath given will he pay him again."

Whilst enjoining the duty of charity on those who are able to extend it, we would encourage those of limited means, to use their strenuous endeavors, by frugality and industry, to maintain themselves and their families, and, by small savings in time of health, to provide for sickness and old age. We would also observe, that the provision made by this society for the relief of the necessitous, was never designed to narrow the duty of charity between individual Friends, nor to lessen the claims which near relatives, in times of necessity, have upon each other. In an especial manner, we esteem it the privilege and the duty of the children of persons who are destitute, to minister to the wants and comfort of their parents, with an affectionate cheerfulness, and not to throw the care of them on others. Those who require pecuniary aid ought to accept the deliberate advice of their friends, as to their outward affairs, and to manifest a becoming disposition to conform therein to their judgment. And where there is an obstinate refusal to conform to such advice, committees should be governed in the distribution of the intended liberality by a prudent discretion.

In order that this concern may be carried into effect, a suitable number of men and women Friends, in each preparative or local meeting, should be annually appointed by each monthly meeting, as overseers of the poor, with liberty to draw on the monthly meeting's treasurer for such funds as may be needed. (*See article on monthly meetings.*) We desire such overseers to proceed with great tenderness towards the feelings of those who are the objects of their appointment, carefully avoiding any unnecessary disclosure of their names, or of the assistance rendered them.

REGULATIONS WITH REGARD TO MARRIAGE.

Persons in membership with us, before they make any procedure with a view to marriage, should seek for right direction in this important concern, and early acquaint their parents or guardians with their intentions; and, having with due deliberation, and free and mutual consent, absolutely contracted upon the account of marriage, they should not be allowed, in any unfaithfulness or injustice one to another, to violate any such engagement.

For the accomplishment of marriage, the parties should inform both the men's and women's monthly meeting to which the woman belongs, of their intentions, (through the preparative meeting when convenient,) that, "With Divine permission and Friends' approbation, they intend marriage with each other." This may be done either by a written communication signed by both parties, or by verbal declaration. Whereupon two Friends in each meeting, (if both the parties belong to the same meeting,) should be appointed, by minute, to make the necessary inquiries respecting the clearness to proceed in marriage, of the party or parties who shall be members of said monthly meeting. If the parties have parents or guardians present, their consent should be expressed; or if the man is a member of another monthly meeting, the consent in writing of his parents or guardians, if he have any, with a certificate from his monthly meeting, of his clearness to proceed therein, should be produced, either then or at the next meeting. If the woman be a widow, having children, two or more Friends should be appointed, to see that the rights of her children are legally secured. At the next meeting, if the committee report that careful inquiry has been made, and that the parties have consent of parents, where it has not been before manifested, and they appear clear to proceed in marriage with each other, the meeting shall leave them at liberty to accomplish their marriage according to our rules. It shall appoint two Friends of each sex, to attend, and see that good order is observed, and that a certificate be prepared, which, after being signed by the parties at their marriage, shall be audibly read; and that a sufficient number of witnesses be thereto subscribed; and the said committee shall make report to the next monthly meeting, and take care that the marriage certificate be duly recorded.

If in any case, a monthly meeting be satisfied, on report of the committee to that effect, or otherwise, that the consent of parents is unreasonably withheld, such meeting is at liberty, in its discretion, to permit proceedings in marriage without such consent.

It is advised that our marriages be solemnized at the usual week day meetings to which the woman belongs, or at the close of a monthly meeting, in a public meeting of men and women Friends, or at such other place and time as may be requested by the parties, or their friends on their behalf, and approved of by the monthly meeting. The parties should be present at the monthly meeting when permission is granted them to accomplish their marriage, if it be their intention to do so at the close of said meeting.

Monthly meetings are at liberty, when they think any peculiarity of circumstances of either of the parties proposing marriage, warrant a deviation from our general practice, to shorten the time of receiving their answer, by adjourning a monthly meeting; having special care that the time for inspecting the clearness of the parties, and receiving the meeting's answer, be not less than two weeks from the time of making their proposals.

Towards the conclusion of the meeting at which the marriage is to be solemnized, the parties should stand up, and, taking each other by the hand, should declare audibly and in a solemn manner, to the following effect, the man first, viz. :

"In the presence of the Lord, and before this assembly, I take thee, D. E., to be my wife; promising, with Divine assistance, to be unto thee a loving and faithful husband, until death shall separate us."

And then the woman in like manner: "In the presence of the Lord, and before this assembly, I take thee, A. B., to be my husband, promising, with Divine assistance, to be unto thee a loving and faithful wife, until death shall separate us.

FORM OF A MARRIAGE CERTIFICATE,

(AS NEAR AS CIRCUMSTANCES WILL ADMIT.)

Whereas, A. B. of ——, son of D. and E. B. of ——, in the county of ——, and state of ——, and S. T. daughter of M. and M. T. of ——, in the county of ——, and state of ——, having declared their intentions of taking each other in marriage, to —— monthly meeting of the Society of Friends, held —— mo. —— A. D. 18—, according to the good order used among them; which, being considered by the said meeting, and no obstruction appearing, they were liberated to accomplish their marriage.

Now, these are to certify to all whom it may concern, that, for the full accomplishing of their said intentions, this —— day of the —— month, in the year of our Lord one thousand eight hundred and ——, they, the said A. B. and S. T. appeared at a religious meeting of the aforesaid society in ——; and he the said A. B. taking the said S. T. by the hand, did openly declare to the following effect: "In the presence of the Lord, and before this assembly, I take thee, S. T., to be my wife, promising, with Divine assistance, to be unto thee a loving and faithful husband, until death shall separate us."

And the said S. T. did then and there declare in like manner: "In the presence of the Lord, and before this assembly, I take thee, A. B., to be my husband, promising, with Divine assistance, to be unto thee a loving and faithful wife, until death shall separate us."

And the said A. B. and S. T., as a further confirmation thereof, have hereunto set their hands, she, after the custom of marriage, adopting the name of her husband.

A. B.
S. B.

And we, whose names are hereunto subscribed, being present at the solemnization of their said marriage, have set our hands as witnesses thereunto, the day and year above written.

No monthly meeting shall permit any marriages to be proposed in the said meeting, sooner than one year after the decease of a former husband or wife; and it is most advisable that no such proposals be made between the parties within that time.

No monthly meeting shall receive proposals of marriage between first cousins, and we earnestly desire all Friends, whenever they know or hear of any first cousins designing or intending to intermarry, that they immediately advise them against it. And, if any, notwithstanding, shall marry contrary to this rule, being previously cautioned and advised against it, the monthly meeting where such belong shall give forth a testimony against them.

When any, who are in the habit of attending our meetings though not in membership with us desire the accomplishment of their marriage according to our rules, the same procedure may be allowed, as when both are members, the monthly meeting noting the fact of non-membership on its records.

RECORDS.

Matters to be Recorded.

1. All meetings for discipline shall keep fair records of the usual minutes of their proceedings, in a suitable book, provided for the purpose.

2. The Yearly Meeting should record all advices, epistles, and conclusions, issued to its subordinate meetings, and to meetings abroad, with which it corresponds; also, a summary of the answers received annually from the quarterly meetings.

3. The quarterly meetings, shall keep a record of advices, epistles, and conclusions, received from the Yearly Meeting, and of all such papers, issued by them to their monthly meetings; also, a summary account of the state of their monthly meetings, compiled from the answers to the queries, once a year.

4. Monthly meetings shall record all advices, epistles, and conclusions, from the Yearly Meeting, or from the quarterly meeting, to which they belong; also, marriages, births, deaths, and burials, marriage certificates, papers of acknowledgment, certificates of removal from or to the meeting, certificates granted to Friends travelling in the ministry, and correspondence with other meetings; also, accounts of sufferings forwarded to the representative meeting.

5. Monthly meetings should appoint a recorder, annually, with an assistant recorder in each preparative meeting, if needed, whose duty it shall be to record all marriages, births, deaths, and burials, marriage certificates, and certificates of removal from or to the meeting. The annexed form of this record, having been found convenient and valuable, is commended to the use of Friends. It is also recommended to monthly meetings, to transcribe their past records into a book of similar form.

Monthly meetings are advised to see that all their record books, and other papers, are carefully collected and preserved; those of earliest date in the older meetings being especially valuable. Much desirable information may be lost for want of care in this respect. Record books should be provided with proper alphabets, that recourse may be had more readily to any particular, when occasion requires.

Our records shall be open to any of our meetings, or individual members, and to such others as the respective monthly meetings shall allow, for the ascertaining of facts relative to marriages, births, or other rights.

If any quarterly meeting requests the records or minutes on any subject of another quarterly meeting, or any monthly meeting those of another monthly meeting, it is directed that copies of such records or minutes be accordingly communicated to the meeting requesting them.

FORM OF RECORD.

NAMES.	RECEIVED.	BORN.	MARRIED.	DISOWNED.	RESTORED.	REMOVED.	RETURNED.	DIED.	AGE.	WHERE BURIED.
William B.	See vol. 1, p. 63.	3 mo. 9, 1790.	} 9 mo. 6, 1818.	......	......	......	......	7 mo. 9, 1850.	60 yrs. 4 mos.	7 mo. 12, 1850, at F——.
C. D. B. (wife)	See p. 37; or by cert. from L., 9 mo. 4, 1820.	8 mo. 7, 1792.		......	......	......	......	......	......	......
Jane, (child,)		9 mo. 4, 1821.	3 mo. 6, 1842 to Y. B.	......	......	See p. 40.	......	......	......	......
Philip,	See p. 53.	3 mo. 4, 1823.	5 mo. 2, 1843, M.C. not a member.	4 mo. 5, 1844.	7 mo. 6, 1846.	......	......	......	......	......
Mary,		9 mo. 7, 1825.	8 mo. 3, 1847, N.O.	......	......	By cert. 10 mo. 11, 1847, to P.	......	......	......	......
——										
R. G.	By request 4 mo. 9, 1840.	......	......	......	......	By cert. 1 mo. 3, 1860, to N.B.	By cert. 2 mo. 9, 1862, from D.	......	......	......

REMOVALS.

When Friends have a prospect of removing, they should be careful not to suffer wrong motives to influence their conclusions; and, before such steps are taken as may close the way of receiving advice, they are advised to take the counsel of some of their experienced Friends, on the propriety of the proposed removal; particularly when they propose removing entirely away from Friends; and elders, and overseers, and other concerned Friends, when they hear of any inclining to remove, should consider it their duty, in brotherly love, to counsel them to observe the foregoing advice.

When a Friend removes, a certificate should be forwarded from the monthly meeting of which he is a member, to the meeting where he is going to reside, expressive only of the right of membership and settlement of temporal concerns, as the case may require — to be founded on inquiry, made by a committee appointed in each case for that purpose; and the committee should not confine their inquiries to the monthly meeting where the person resides, if there be reason to believe that his affairs are not settled elsewhere. If the certificate be for an acknowledged minister, or elder, it should so state. It being obviously important that such recommendation should take place without unnecessary delay, in order that the individual may come under the early notice and oversight of the meeting within the limits of which he removes, if the Friend does not himself apply for a certificate, within six months from the time of his removal, the monthly meeting should forward one for him, without such application.

When a certificate of removal is received by the meeting to which it is directed, it shall be the duty of that meeting to accept it, unless there be some manifest obstruction; and, when accepted, the Friend recommended by it shall be a member of that meeting.

Removal certificates should be forwarded for apprentices and others under age, who are placed within the limits of another monthly meeting.

When a meeting accepts a certificate, it should inform the meeting which issued it, of such acceptance.

All certificates of removal, issued by our monthly meetings, should be signed by the clerks of both the men's and women's meetings.

No Friend shall gain a settlement by marriage certificate or other recommendation, unless a removal be expressed therein.

DIFFERENCES AND ARBITRATIONS.

It is advised that in all cases of controversy and difference, the persons concerned therein either speedily adjust the difference between themselves, or make choice of some faithful, disinterested, impartial Friends, to determine the same; and that all Friends avoid taking sides in any personal controversy or differences, and it would be well that Friends were at all times ready to submit their differences, even with persons not of our religious persuasion, to arbitration rather than to contend at law. "Hear the causes between your brethren, and judge righteously between every man and his brother, and the stranger that is with him."

It is advised that persons differing about outward things do, as little as may be, trouble ministering Friends in any respect, in relation thereto.

If any Friend shall refuse speedily to end a difference in which he is a party concerned, or to refer it, as before advised, or shall fail to appoint an arbitrator within the period of one month after notice to do so has been given him, by the overseers or other Friends who have advised him to refer it, the case should be referred to the monthly meeting to which the Friend belongs; and if such meeting also judges that the case ought to be so referred, and the Friend shall still refuse to refer it, or fail to appoint an arbitrator without further delay, the monthly meeting, after the exercise of due care, and with a just regard to the interests of all parties, shall express its disunity with his conduct, and may proceed to disown him as a member of our society.

When cases of difference are referred, and judgment and award are made, signed, and given thereupon, the parties concerned shall stand to and perform the said award; and, if any one shall refuse so to do, the monthly meeting to which such person belongs, upon notice to it given, shall admonish him thereto, and if, after admonition, he persists to refuse, the meeting may then proceed to disownment.

The rules for the settlement of differences about property shall not be considered as binding upon trustees and executors, acting for others, in the performance of their duties as such; nor upon any Friends acting on behalf of persons not of our religious society, and so as to incur a legal responsibility to them.

Matters of defamation are not subjects to be arbitrated, until the defamation is proved, as well as the fact that some injury is sustained by the defamed, in his trade or property; and, in that case, the damage should be submitted to arbitration.

MODE OF CONDUCTING ARBITRATIONS.

Each party having chosen one or two indifferent, impartial, and judicious Friends, those so chosen shall agree upon a third or a fifth Friend, (unless the parties first agree in the nomination,) whose name shall be inserted with the others, in the bonds of arbitration or other written agreement.

The arbitrators, so appointed, or the majority of them, shall fix the time and place of their first meeting, within three months after their appointment. At the hearing, all the arbitrators shall be present and act.

The arbitrators shall not consider themselves as advocates for the party by whom they are chosen, but men whose incumbent duty it is to judge righteously, fearing the Lord. They shall shun all previous information respecting the case, and especially avoid any bias in their judgments, before they hear both parties together.

The parties shall enter into written agreements, if either of them require it, to abide by the award of the arbitrators, or a majority of them, to be made in a limited time, and it would be well that this agreement should be in the form of a rule of court, duly authenticated, so that, if occasion should require it, the award may be legally enforced, without resort to a suit at law. And, in the event of a failure of either party to abide by such award, monthly meetings may, in their discretion, give permission to enforce the same, should a resort to law become necessary.

Every meeting of the arbitrators shall be duly made known to the parties concerned, until they have been fully heard; and there should not be any separate or private meetings, between some of the arbitrators, or with one party separate from the other, on the business referred to them; and no representation of the case of one party, either by writing, or otherwise, shall be admitted, without its being fully made known to the other, and, if required, a copy shall be delivered to the other party.

The arbitrators shall hear both parties fully, in the presence of each other, whilst either has any fresh matter to offer, until a certain time, to be limited by the arbitrators. Let no evidence or witness, pertinent to the case, be rejected or withheld.

If there should appear to the arbitrators, or to one or more of them, to be any doubtful point of law, the majority of them shall agree upon a case, and consult counsel thereupon. The arbitrators are not required to express, in the award, the reasons for their decision. When the arbitrators do not act under a rule of a court, a copy of the award shall be delivered to each party.

Arbitrators should propose to the parties that they give an acknowledgment in writing, before the award be made, that they have been candidly and fully heard.

APPEALS.

If any person shall, after a final decision in his case, by any monthly meeting, think himself injured or aggrieved by its proceedings, he may appeal to the quarterly meeting, of which such monthly meeting forms a part.

Notice of such intended appeal must be given in writing to the monthly meeting, within three months after such decision is communicated, by, or on behalf of, such meeting, to the party concerned.

When an appeal is made to the quarterly meeting, by any person dissatisfied with the proceedings of the monthly meeting, the quarterly meeting shall proceed to nominate a committee of seven disinterested Friends, to hear the same and judge thereof. The appellant should not be present, and no member of the monthly meeting appealed from, should be at liberty to take any part in nominating the committee of the quarterly meeting, neither should any member of said monthly meeting be appointed thereon.

After the nomination has taken place, the appellant shall be called in, and the names of the proposed committee shall be read in his presence, and each party shall have the liberty of objecting to any part of the committee, not exceeding three, and the places of those objected to shall be supplied by other nominations being made; which nominations shall be final.

The committee shall then withdraw and hear the parties concerned in the appeal, and the appellant shall have the liberty of taking with him one or two of his friends, to assist him in the management of his case; and, when the committee have come to judgment in regard to it, they shall prepare a report of their decision, signed by those uniting in judgment, as the report of the committee. If the report in the case of the disownment of any person be signed by less than two-thirds of the committee, the appellant shall be restored to membership.

If any person shall think himself aggrieved by the judgment of any quarterly meeting, he may appeal from such judgment to the Yearly Meeting; in which case, notice in writing, of his intention to appeal, shall be given by him, not later than the second quarterly meeting after that at which such judgment has been recorded.

If any appellant or appellants do not bring his, her, or their appeal to the Yearly Meeting next ensuing, due notice once given them, if such appellants continue their appeal, notice shall be repeated, in writing, to the meeting against which they may appeal, at least three months preceding the Yearly Meeting.

When the appeal from the judgment of the quarterly meeting shall have been read in the Yearly Meeting, a committee of disinterested Friends, consisting of two from each quarterly meeting, except the meeting appealed from, shall be appointed; and no member of said quarterly meeting shall take part in the nomination of said committee. The appellant shall then be called in, and the names of the committee shall be read in his presence; and each party shall have the liberty of objecting to any member of the committee, thus nominated, not exceeding five; and the vacancies thus made shall be filled by other nominations, which shall be final.

The committee shall then withdraw and hear the parties concerned, and the appellant shall have the liberty of taking with him two or three of his friends, to assist him in the management of his case.

When, in the committee, the whole or the greater part of them have agreed in a judgment of the case, a report in writing shall be prepared, which shall be signed, as the report of the committee, by those so uniting in judgment. If the report of a committee in the case of a disownment of any person, be signed by less than two-thirds of their number, the judgment of the quarterly meeting shall be reversed, and the appellant restored to the rights of membership.

The committee shall not be expected to assign any reasons for the judgment expressed in their report; and it is recommended that such report be simply the confirming or annulling of the decision of the quarterly meeting, unless it be annulled for irregular dealing, in which case it should be so expressed.

When the personal rights of a member under dealing are affected by nonconformity to the discipline, or by other irregularity in the proceedings, the decision in the case, if he be disowned, shall, on appeal therefrom, be reversed for that cause; but monthly meetings shall have the right, when their decisions are reversed on account of irregular dealing *only*, to take up the case again, and proceed according to the discipline, the same as if it had not already been acted upon.

Appeals to the Yearly Meeting, shall be entered and acted upon, on the second day of the week.

TRUST PROPERTY.

In the tenure and management of property, held in trust, or otherwise, monthly meetings should observe the following course.

Particular care should be taken by the proper and respective meetings concerned, that all title deeds and writings relating to meeting-houses, burial-grounds, and trust property of any kind, held for the use of our society, or for any part thereof, as well as all deeds and records relative to donations, and legacies, be deposited in a place of security; and that the custody of them be entrusted to two or more of the overseers of the monthly meeting, or to other Friends appointed for that purpose.

In the acceptance of trusts, monthly meetings are desired to be very careful that the trust proposed does not, in any way, do injustice to those who have a reasonable expectation from their kindred or near connections.[*]

Executors and trustees, concerned in wills and settlements, are advised to take special care that they faithfully discharge their respective trusts according to the intent of the donors and testators; that all charitable gifts, legacies, bequests, donations, and settlements of estates, by will or deed, intended or given for the use or benefit of the poor, for education, or for promoting the cause of morality and religion, or for any purpose consistent with our moral and religious principles, be not converted or

[*] See article on Temporal Affairs.

appropriated to any other use than that directed and enjoined by the donors and testators; and should any unforseen occurrence render such performance difficult or impracticable, early application should be made to the Representative meeting for its advice or assistance.

And, in order that it may appear, not only now, but in all future time, that all gifts and legacies have been properly and strictly applied, according to the intention and direction of the donors and testators, monthly meetings or other meetings concerned, should take special care, annually, to know that proper books are kept by the trustees in which are recorded as follows, viz.

First, — the will or clauses, with the date of probate thereof; — or the title deed, with the date of the record thereof; — or any other writing by which trust property of any kind is conveyed.

Second, — the place of deposit of such will, deed, or conveyance.

Third, — the names of the trustees.

Fourth, — an inventory or exhibit of the trust property.

Fifth, — a regular and systematic account of all incomes and disbursements of said property.

Sixth, — that an annual exhibit of the state of the funds or property be made therefrom for the donees; and a settlement be made with them, when competent thereto, by the outgoing trustees, and also for the acceptance of the incoming trustees.

Seventh, — that a clear and correct account may be open at all times to the donees, and such others as may have right to know the state thereof; and also to the courts, if it should be required.

When the trust property belongs to preparative or particular meetings, the monthly meeting should exercise the same care and jurisdiction as in all other cases.

Overseers are not at liberty to accept trusts by will, donation, or otherwise, until they are directed to do so by the monthly meeting; and they shall be subject to the direction of the monthly meeting in the management, or disposition, of such trusts or other property.

When the trust property belongs to any distinct body or committee of Friends, or is under their care, as in the case of schools and other charitable foundations, it is recommended that the spirit of the above rules should be attended to, and the provisions be complied with, as far as circumstances will permit.

Should any meeting be dissolved, or cease to retain its distinct character, care should be taken, that a minute be previously entered on its books for regularly transferring the property under its direction, to the superintendence of the meeting which may succeed it in its authority or rights, in all instances, where the nature of the trust admits of this being done.

INTOXICATING LIQUORS, TOBACCO, &c.

All our members are cautioned carefully to avoid the distillation, importation, trading in, or in any way using, or encouraging the use in others, of all intoxicating liquors. And if any of our members shall be found in either of these practices, monthly meetings should labor with all such, and endeavor to prevail with them to a cordial compliance with the advice here given; and if, notwithstanding, any continue therein, they should be testified against.

We also recommend to all our members to abstain from the use of tobacco, opium, and other narcotic substances or preparations.

DEFAMATION AND DETRACTION.

Friends are admonished to stand upon their guard against all whispering, backbiting, and evil speaking one of another, and to discourage every practice of that nature, observing the advice of the apostle, "Let all bitterness, and wrath, and anger, and clamor, and evil-speaking, be put away from you, with all malice: and be ye kind one to another, tender-hearted, forgiving one another, even as God for Christ's sake hath forgiven you," Eph. iv. 31, 32; always mindful of the precept of our Lord, "Whatsoever ye would that men should do to you, do ye even so to them." Matt. vii. 12.

"Charity," saith the apostle, "hopeth all things." It divulges not the faults of others, because, in its unbounded hope, it desires their removal without exposure. For the mind in which it dwells, ascribes its own preservation and the cleansing of its former sins, to the unbounded love of God in Christ Jesus, and it prays that all may partake of the same benefit. How opposite that disposition which delights to report evil, and to accuse! Shun it, dear Friends, as the poison of asps. The sacred writings emphatically denominate the grand adversary of mankind by the name of the accuser of the brethren. "Follow," therefore, "peace with all men, and holiness, without which no man shall see the Lord: looking diligently, lest any man fail of the grace of God; lest any root of bitterness springing up, trouble you, and thereby many be defiled."

If, however, any person be charged with defamation or scandal, he should be proceeded against in the manner and by the several steps following:

First, the person defamed, or supposed to be defamed, himself, or any other Friend to whom the knowledge of the case shall come, should go to the accused, and tell him his fault, or supposed fault, between them alone, and, by the best method he is capable of, labor to convince him of it, in order to his acknowledgment of the truth, and to his repentance, if he appear to be guilty. But, if the accused shall refuse to make such satisfaction as the nature of the case requires, let the accuser take with him one or two Friends of the monthly meeting to which the accused belongs, if it may be conveniently done; and if the accused think fit, he may bring with him one or two Friends also of the same monthly meeting; and they, together, shall endeavor to obtain the true knowledge of the case, by hearing witnesses, if there be occasion. And, if they all judge him guilty, and he doth not make satisfaction; or, if they do not all agree that he is innocent; in either of these cases happening, the person charging is at liberty to bring the matter before the monthly meeting, which is the only judge now remaining, both of the nature of the fact, and the validity of the proof of it; and Friends in the wisdom of God, shall deal with him for the good ends before mentioned; and, as they see cause, upon mature and deliberate consideration, shall justify or condemn him. And, if the church shall see meet to commit the consideration of a case of this nature, for better dispatch, to certain persons of its own body, we recommend it as our tender advice, in case the accused shall object against one or more of the Friends so chosen, that the church have due regard to such objection, and set aside the person or persons so objected against, and substitute another or others in his or their room, provided such objection doth not extend to the major part of the Friends so chosen. And, in general, we desire all tenderness and regard may be had to a person under such circumstances; and that Friends in a spirit of love and condescension, deal with such, keeping up at the same time the authority of their meetings.

If any Friend hear an injurious report of another, he should discountenance it, by showing the reporter the evil and injustice of spreading such reports; and then, without further spreading it, if it appear expedient, he should go to the person whom it concerns, or advise him of it, that he may have opportunity to clear himself if innocent, or to make satisfaction if guilty; and should this private labor prove ineffectual, the overseers should be informed, that he may be treated with, consistently with our discipline.

Any one circulating a report, injurious to another, and refusing to give his authority for the same, should be held responsible, as the author thereof, and be dealt with accordingly.

INDEX.

₊ *The large capitals denote the headings of chapters, the smaller capitals the headings of sections.*

Acceptance of Certificates of Removal 127
Aborigines, Concern relating to 60
Absent members, Correspondence with 88
Accounts, Prompt settlement of 52
ADVICE IN RELATION TO MARRIAGE 49
ADVICE IN RELATION TO TEMPORAL AFFAIRS 51
ADVICE IN RELATION TO THE MINISTRY 34
ADVICES, GENERAL 100
ADVICES TO BE READ IN MEETINGS OF MINISTERS AND ELDERS 114
Affirmations, Caution respecting 61
AMUSEMENTS AND RECREATIONS 54
APPEALS 130
   to Quarterly Meetings 130
   to the Yearly Meeting 131, 133
   Proceedings in relation to..131, 132
Attendance of Meetings 17
Auditors, Appointment of 86

BENEVOLENCE AND LIBERALITY 32
Births, Deaths, &c., to be recorded... 123
BOOKS 41
   Pernicious 42, 46
   provided for distribution 116
Book of Discipline to be present in Meetings for Discipline 74
BURIAL AND MOURNING HABITS 65
Burial Grounds 65, 66

CARE OF THE POOR 117
Certificates of Marriage, Form of.... 121
   to Travelling Ministers 96
   of Removal 126
   on account of Marriage 119
Children, Parents' care for 42, 45

CHRISTIAN DOCTRINE 1
   PRACTICE 16
   DISCIPLINE 67
CIVIL GOVERNMENT 61
   Office, Holding of 62, 93
Complaints against members 99, 100
Convinced Persons to be visited..... 24
Correspondents 85
Counsel to attendance of Meetings for Worship 16, 19
   against self-indulgence and a worldly spirit 25, 26, 33
   to exercise of forbearance and forgiveness 32
   to Ministers and Elders 34, 38
   to Parents and Guardians 42
   TO THE YOUNG 45
   against joint securities with others 51
   against too eager pursuit of riches 52
   to avoid vain sports and pastimes 55
   against joining secret societies. 91
   to the poor and such as are in straitened circumstances 117, 118
   against the use of intoxicating liquors, &c. 135
   to avoid detraction and evil speaking 136
COVETOUSNESS 66
DEFAMATION AND DETRACTION 136
   Proceedings in case of 136
DELINQUENCIES — how treated 90, 91
   Defrauding the Revenue 91
   Aiding in warlike matters 92
   Military Pensions 92
   Failing to pay just Debts 92

INDEX.

Absenting from Religious Meetings.. 93
Printing, publishing, or circulating hurtful works.......... 93
Accepting certain offices...... 93
Arresting or suing members... 93
Attending improper places, immoralities, &c................. 94
Joining Secret Societies........ 94
Refusing to Arbitrate or abide by award of Arbitrators..... 128
Making, using, or trafficking in intoxicating liquors.......... 135
Detraction............................. 136
DIFFERENCES AND ARBITRATIONS.. 127
General Regulations............ 128
not binding on Trustees, &c., in certain cases............... 128
Conducting of Arbitrations.... 129
DISCIPLINE, CHRISTIAN............. 67
Historical sketch of............ 67
Meetings for Discipline........ 71
Drowsiness in Meetings............. 18

Economy in Living..................33, 52
EDUCATION............................ 38
Choice of Books................ 40
Elders, Qualifications of............ 97
Appointment of................ 97
Displacement of................ 98
ELDERS AND MINISTERS............. 110
Executors and Administrators....... 54

Families, Committees to visit........ 89
FASTS AND REJOICINGS............... 63
FIRST DAY OF THE WEEK, ON THE RIGHT OCCUPATION OF......... 56
Form of Record of Births, &c....... 125
of Marriage Certificate.......... 121

GENERAL ADVICES 100
GIFTS AND SERVICES FOR THE RELIGIOUS BENEFIT OF OTHERS..... 23
Gravestones......................... 65
Guardians, Designation of........... 54
and Parents.................... 42

Holy Days, So called............... 63
HOLY SCRIPTURES.................... 14
ON READING THE............22, 57
Insolvency, Advice respecting...... 52
INTOXICATING LIQUORS, TOBACCO, &C.................................. 135

LOVE AND UNITY, PART I............ 28
PART II........... 31
LIBERALITY AND BENEVOLENCE.... 32
MARRIAGE, ADVICE IN RELATION TO 49
Regulations 119
deviations from Rules, When allowed...................... 120
certificate, Form of........121, 122
between first cousins disallowed............................. 122
with persons not in membership........................... 122
MEETINGS FOR WORSHIP............. 16
MEETINGS FOR DISCIPLINE.......... 71
Subordination of............... 73
Members, Lists of to be kept........ 88
absent, To be corresponded with........................... 88
Proceedings in cases of Admission, Resignation or Exclusion of......................... 89
Membership, Who entitled to........ 87
what minors may be admitted to.............................. 87
Requests for admission to....87, 99
Resignation of.................88, 89
MEMORIALS 98
Ministers, Recognition of............ 94
causing dissatisfaction.......... 95
certificates for travelling...... 96
MINISTERS AND ELDERS.............. 110
Displacement of................. 111
Disowned, If restored do not thereby regain their standing 110
MINISTERS AND ELDERS, MEETINGS OF 111
Preparative Meetings of....... 111
Quarterly Meetings of.......... 112
List of its Members to be annually revised................ 112
Yearly Meeting of.............. 113
Queries to be read in.......... 113
Advices to be read in.......... 114
To present Summary Account to Yearly Meeting annually.. 113
MINISTRY, ADVICE RELATING TO THE 34
MONTHLY MEETINGS................. 85
Organization of................ 85
How laid down.................. 85
Appointments to be annually made........................... 86
Lists of members............... 88
Admission, disowning or dismissal of members to be by concurrent action............. 89

INDEX. 141

Visiting Committees............ 89
    Delinquencies................ 90
Ministers, Acknowledgment of..... 94
    Elders, Appointment of....... 97
Months and Days, Names of........ 64
Mothers, Counsel to.............. 43
MOURNING HABITS AND BURIALS... 65

Names of Months and Days of the week.......................... 64

OATHS 60, 92
Overseers, Appointment of......... 85
    Duties of....................86, 109
Overseers of the Poor...........86, 118
OVERSIGHT 106, 110
Offenders, Dealing with...........90, 95
    Contributions not to be received from persons under dealing.. 74

PARENTS AND GUARDIANS.......... 42
Payment of war taxes.............59, 92
Pensions for military services........ 92
Pernicious Books, Caution against.. 42
POOR, CARE OF THE................ 117
    Overseers of.................86, 118
PREPARATIVE MEETINGS............ 99
    Duties of...................... 99
    small, May be held jointly..... 100
    when dispensed with.......... 100
    complaints by Overseers....99, 100
PRIVATE RETIREMENT AND PRAYER 20
QUARTERLY MEETINGS.............. 82
    Time of holding................ 82
QUERIES.......................... 103
    of Meetings of Ministers and Elders..................... 113
Requests for Membership......87, 89, 99
Resignations of Membership........88, 89
REPRESENTATIVE MEETING.......... 115
    How appointed................ 115
    Members to send excuse for non-attendance 115
    to take oversight of publications relating to our religious principles........................ 93

Representatives...........81, 85, 86, 100
    not to withdraw without leave 81
RECORDS 123
    Form of...................... 125
REMOVALS.......................... 126
READING THE HOLY SCRIPTURES ... 22

Settlement of Accounts, Frequent.. 52
Scriptural Instruction recommended 24, 41, 57
SIMPLICITY, MODERATION AND SELF-DENIAL 26
SLAVERY AND OPPRESSION.......... 59

Testimonies concerning Friends deceased............................ 98
TEMPORAL AFFAIRS, ADVICE RELATING TO........................ 51
Tobacco, Opium, &c................ 135
Travelling, Certificates for Ministers 96
Trust Property...................... 133
    Course in relation to........... 133
    Custody of Deeds, Records, &c. 133
    To be applied to purposes intended by the Donors........ 133
Trustee Books, how kept........... 134
    Overseers subject to Monthly Meetings in accepting and managing Trusts............. 135
    Case of Meetings dissolved.... 135

UNANSWERED QUERIES..........106, 114

Visiting Families................... 89

WAR.............................. 58
    Taxes for support of..........59, 92
    Pursuits connected with........ 92
    Procuring Substitutes.......... 92
Wills, Advice respecting..........53, 54
Womens' Meetings,..............72, 73, 74

YEARLY MEETING, Its History.... 75
    Design and Functions.......... 80
    Regulations.................... 80
    Appointment of Clerks........ 81
    Collections for Expenses...... 81

B

www.ingramcontent.com/pod-product-compliance
Lightning Source LLC
Chambersburg PA
CBHW030344170426
43202CB00010B/1232